Elizabeth

Elizabeth

Her Life, Our Times

ALAN TITCHMARSH

1 3 5 7 9 10 8 6 4 2

First published in 2012 by BBC Books, an imprint of Ebury Publishing.
A Random House Group Company. The paperback edition published in 2013.

The Random House Group Limited Reg. No. 954009

Addresses for companies within the Random House Group can be found at
www.randomhouse.co.uk

A CIP catalogue record for this book is available from the British Library.

ISBN: 978 1 849 90665 4

Commissioning editor: Lorna Russell
Project editor: Joe Cottington
Copy editor: Imogen Fortes
Designer: Seagull Design
Picture researcher: Claire Gouldstone
Production: Antony Heller

Printed and bound in the UK by CPI Group (UK) Ltd, Croydon, CR0 4YY

To buy books by your favourite authors and register for offers visit
www.randomhouse.co.uk

CONTENTS

INTRODUCTION

Despite numerous biographies, many of them meticulously researched and drawing on interviews with those who know her, Queen Elizabeth the Second, by the Grace of God, Queen of the United Kingdom of Great Britain and Northern Ireland and Her other Realms and Territories, Head of the Commonwealth, Defender of the Faith, remains something of an enigma. It is a state of affairs that, in its own way, contributes to her status as sovereign. One of the most famous opinions ever expressed on the monarchy is that of the Victorian constitutional expert Walter Bagehot who wrote: "Its mystery is its life. We must not let in daylight to take away its magic." The wisdom of this oft-quoted remark was demonstrated – albeit metaphorically – in The Queen's famous 'annus horribilis' of 1992, which culminated in the devastating fire at Windsor Castle caused by a spotlight setting fire to a curtain. It is unlikely that the irony was lost on Her Majesty.

The Queen has never granted an interview. Any knowledge that the majority of her people have of her character and personality must be provided at second hand by those who have encountered her or worked with her. And there seems to be no shortage of those who would attempt to cast light upon the life of one of the most famous women in the world who, on 6 February 2012, celebrated her Diamond Jubilee and became the second longest-serving monarch in our history after Queen Victoria, who reigned for 63 years 216 days.

It is said that The Queen keeps a diary. How much of herself she reveals within its pages we may never know – at least not in her lifetime. But we *can* learn from the part of her annual record that she shares with us each year in December when she makes her Christmas broadcast to the nation.

'The Queen's Christmas Message' may sometimes seem relatively anodyne or slightly stilted, but an examination of all of them (including the only written message, in 1969, when the film *Royal Family* was transmitted and a separate broadcast message was considered unnecessary) reveals more about Her Majesty as a person than might at first be apparent. The broadcasts also demonstrate, on many occasions, her remarkable foresight.

The Queen's roles as monarch, wife, mother and head of state are all touched upon in these messages, and from the very first of her broadcasts – transmitted live from her Norfolk home, Sandringham, at 3.07 p.m. on Christmas Day 1952 – we are given a measured insight into The Queen's feelings.

For 60 years she has presided over Great Britain and those other 'Realms and Territories' that form something called the 'Commonwealth' – what remains of Queen Victoria's British Empire. Few would argue that Queen Elizabeth II has not done it with an unfailing sense of dedication and duty.

On the tragic death of Diana, Princess of Wales, in August 1997, when The Queen, as head of the family, remained at Balmoral in Scotland with her grandsons, one tabloid newspaper, reflecting the general mood that The Queen should be in London with her people, emblazoned its front page with the words: "SHOW US YOU CARE MA'AM". For a woman who has spent all her adult life caring for the 200 million people of her native country and the Commonwealth, the remark must have been especially wounding at a time when she considered that those who most needed her care – away from the prying eyes of the world's media – were her two young grandsons. It was a reminder that despite the trappings of royalty and the rarefied atmosphere of any palace The Queen is a human being – a wife, mother and grandmother – with human frailties and human sensibilities. While seemingly 'above it all' and rarely able to express an opinion, it would be a mistake to assume that she does not have opinions, or that she regards herself as being socially superior to the rest of us. Quite the contrary. The Queen once remarked of a particularly aristocratic family that they were "far too grand for us".

In her speech at Guildhall to mark the 40th anniversary of her accession – the 'annus horribilis' speech – The Queen remarked:

> It is possible to have too much of a good thing. A well-meaning bishop was obviously doing his best when he told Queen Victoria, 'Ma'am, we cannot pray too often, nor too fervently, for the Royal Family.' The Queen's reply was: 'Too fervently, no; too often, yes.' I, like Queen Victoria, have always been a believer in that old maxim, 'moderation in all things.

Except, it seems, devotion to her people.

You might wonder how a man who is best known as a gardener, a novelist, a broadcaster and a presenter of television and radio programmes on subjects as diverse as horticulture and music is qualified to pen a record of his monarch's 60-year reign. My excuse is not just the obvious one that I have lived all but three years of my life under her rule, and that like every one of her subjects I have carried her image in the change in my pocket and stuck stamps bearing her profile on a lifetime's worth of envelopes. Neither is it simply that I have enormous respect for her achievements and deep admiration of the way in which she has devoted herself to her subjects over six decades. That much is true. But I have also had the good fortune and privilege to meet Her Majesty on many occasions, both official and social. I have planted a tree with her, shown her a garden I have made, sat next to her at lunch; and while I would never claim to be even a distant part of her wide social circle, on that particular occasion I found to my surprise and delight that The Queen was prepared to converse relatively freely on a wide range of subjects. Like her dedicated and devoted ladies-in-waiting, I am unwilling to reveal all that was said. One of the most underestimated qualities in life is that of keeping a confidence. But these encounters, along with my meetings and interviews with other members of the royal family have given me at least an inkling of what they are about.

I am an avid reader, and for many years my shelves have contained most of the biographies written about The Queen, and many about the lives of her forebears, from Henry VIII and Elizabeth I to Charles I, George III and the unfortunate Duke of Windsor. I like books; their information is generally more reliable than that found in many places on the internet, and once written they remain free of interference.

What follows is not, I hope, an unqualified paean of praise, neither is it solely based on a series of interviews with those who know her or work with her – though I have talked over the years to nearly every member of her family, and to friends and staff. Such recollections will play their part. This is above all a record of Queen Elizabeth the Second's reign and a reflection of the changes that have taken place in our own lives over that period, taking as a springboard the words of The Queen herself, as broadcast to the people to whom she has given a lifetime of service. By looking at Her Majesty's annual Christmas messages over the past six decades, as I will in this book, we can perhaps learn more from her own sentiments than we ever could from idle gossip and shrieking newspaper headlines.

If I am too ready to praise The Queen and the closest members of her family, it is only because I have observed at close quarters how hard they work and just how selfless is their dedication and loyalty to their country and to their people – both as a nation and as individuals. It seems to me more important to make judgements of the royal family's worth based on that premise than on the misfortunes and vicissitudes of their marital relationships. In the words of The Queen herself, in that speech at Guildhall in 1992:

> *There can be no doubt, of course, that criticism is good for people and institutions that are part of public life. No institution – City, Monarchy, whatever – should expect to be free from the scrutiny of those who give it their loyalty and support, not to mention those who don't. But we are all part of the same fabric of our national society and that scrutiny, by one part of another, can be just as effective if it is made with a touch of gentleness, good humour and understanding.*

This book, I hope, contains all three in equal measure.

God Save The Queen.

Alan Titchmarsh

"A fair and youthful figure, Princess, wife and mother, is the heir to all our traditions and glories never greater than in her father's days, and to all our perplexities and dangers never greater in peacetime than now. She is also heir to all our united strength and loyalty.

"She comes to the Throne at a time when tormented mankind stands uncertainly poised between world catastrophe and a golden age. That it should be a golden age of art and letters, we can only hope – science and machinery have their tales to tell – but it is certain that if a true and lasting peace can be achieved, and if the nations will only let each other alone, an immense and undreamed of prosperity with culture and leisure ever more widely spread can come, perhaps even easily and swiftly, to the masses of people in every land.

"Let us hope and pray that the accession to our ancient Throne of Queen Elizabeth the Second may be the signal for such a brightening salvation of the human scene."

WINSTON CHURCHILL, HOUSE OF COMMONS,
11 FEBRUARY 1952

THE ACCESSION

"I declare before you all that my whole life whether it be long or short shall be devoted to your service and the service of our great imperial family to which we all belong. But I shall not have strength to carry out this resolution alone unless you join in it with me, as I now invite you to do. I know that your support will be unfailingly given. God help me to make good my vow, and God bless all of you who are willing to share in it."

PRINCESS ELIZABETH'S 21ST BIRTHDAY BROADCAST

Princess Elizabeth, daughter of The Duke and Duchess of York, knew from the age of 11 years and 8 months that provided her parents did not give birth to a son she would one day become the Queen of England. Her uncle, King Edward VIII, known to the family as David, signed the Instrument of Abdication on 10 December 1936 at Fort Belvedere, his home in Surrey, in order to marry "the woman I love" – twice-divorced American Wallis Warfield Simpson. His government had made it clear that he must choose between the love of a constitutionally unacceptable woman or that of his country. He chose the woman. His reign effectively ended the following day, making him the fifth shortest-reigning monarch in British history, at 326 days.

The coronation, planned for the following year, did take place, but the crown was not placed upon the head of the man whose own father, King George V, had worried would not be up to the job. It was placed, instead, upon the head of his younger brother, Prince Albert (Bertie to his family), who was crowned King George VI, his fourth Christian name, chosen to provide stability and continuity.

Edward left the country immediately upon abdicating, and married "that woman", Wallis Simpson, in France on 3 June 1937. They became The Duke and Duchess of Windsor, though the prefix 'Her Royal Highness' was famously denied to the former King's wife – a source of bitter regret to her husband who, until his death in exile in 1972, found it hard to forgive his family for their perceived cold-heartedness.

From the moment of Edward's abdication, the life of his brother and his brother's family was dramatically altered, thanks to the line of succession.

Prince Albert, Duke of York, had married Elizabeth Bowes-Lyon, daughter of The Earl of Strathmore and Kinghorne, on 26 April 1923. The future Duchess of York, having turned down her future husband's first two proposals, finally acquiesced at his third attempt. Their first child, Princess Elizabeth Alexandra Mary, was born at her maternal grandparents' London home, 17 Bruton Street in London's Mayfair, on 21 April 1926, and her sister Princess Margaret Rose at the Strathmores' Scottish seat, Glamis Castle, on 21 August 1930. In their early years, both children might have hoped that to some extent they could lead a relatively 'normal' life away from the spotlight's glare – that being the province of the future king, their Uncle David – but in 1936 everything changed.

The shock of those terrible December days was literally stunning said the late Queen Mother, who recalled that in the months immediately afterwards she felt

> *as if I was coming to after a heavy blow on the head.*

THE EARLY YEARS

Queen Elizabeth II can trace her ancestry back to Egbert, who was King of England from 827 to 839. She is Queen Victoria's great, great-grandchild and our 40th monarch since William the Conqueror. She was brought up with Princess Margaret Rose (as she was always known in childhood) at 145 Piccadilly (subsequently flattened by a bomb during the Second World War), and the family spent their summer holidays at Birkhall near the private Scottish residence of the royal family at Balmoral in Aberdeenshire. From 1931 onwards King George V gave the family the use of Royal Lodge in Windsor Great Park as their country home, added to which they would spend time with their two sets of grandparents – with The King and Queen at Sandringham and Balmoral, and The Earl and Countess of Strathmore at Glamis Castle and St Paul's Walden Bury in Hertfordshire. Given the amount of time the young Elizabeth spent in the British countryside it is not surprising that Windsor Great Park is still preferred to The Mall, and that her lifelong passions have been those of horses and dogs.

The young Princesses did not go to school, but were taught at home by a governess – a Scottish schoolteacher, Marion Crawford, known as 'Crawfie' and revered by the family whom she served for 17 years until, in 1950, she breached their confidence by publishing *The Little Princesses*, revealing secrets of their royal home life. Relatively inoffensive though these confidences appear to be today, the perceived breach of trust was to result in her falling from grace.

The girls' nanny, Clara Wright (always known as 'Alah' – pronounced 'Arla'), committed no such solecism, and along with Crawfie presided over the girls' walks in the park, their learning to read and their piano lessons. As Marion Crawford wrote in *The Little Princesses*:

> *Alah had entire charge in those days of the children's out-of-school lives – their health, their baths, their clothes – while I had them from nine to six. She had to help her an under-nurse and a nursemaid.*

The under-nurse was Margaret Macdonald, known as 'Bobo', who was to serve Queen Elizabeth II for 67 years – most of them as The Queen's dresser – until she died aged 89 in 1993. She was, according to Ben Pimlott, "scourge of designers and milliners, relentless custodian, daily companion, confidante and friend".

The young Princess learned to speak French, among other accomplishments, and the future Queen's love of horses was in evidence from an early age, with many games revolving

Elizabeth and Margaret Rose enjoyed an idyllic childhood, slowly adjusting to the realities of King Edward VIII's abdication.

WITH BEST WISHES FOR
CHRISTMAS AND THE NEW YEAR

A 1964 Christmas card, signed by Prince Philip and 'Lilibet'.

around Margaret Rose being 'harnessed' and driven around the nursery by her older sister, who has been known to her intimates from those early days as Lilibet – the pet name given to her by her grandfather, King George V. The Queen still signs herself thus to her family and close friends.

On the accession of their father, Princesses Elizabeth and Margaret Rose moved from 145 Piccadilly to Buckingham Palace where the extensive grounds and lake provided a new playground. When the threat of invasion became serious during the Second World War, The King and Queen remained in the palace but sent their children to Windsor, both King and Queen rejecting the idea that they should all move overseas. As the then Queen remarked:

The children won't go without me. I won't leave The King. And The King will never leave.

During the war, Elizabeth, by now a teenager, helped the war effort by rolling bandages and knitting socks, and towards the end of the conflict joined the Auxiliary Territorial Service (ATS) where she drove and mended military vehicles. At the end of the war, on VE Day, 8 May 1945, when The King and Queen appeared on the balcony of Buckingham Palace accompanied by the wartime Prime Minister Winston Churchill, they waved at a huge enthusiastic crowd. That crowd contained their own daughters, who had ventured out to mingle anonymously with the throng, anxious to be a part of the people's celebration.

The King and Queen remained exceptionally close to their daughters – The King referring to the family as "we four" – and George VI passed on his own sense of duty to his daughter, making sure that she had a rigorous education in matters constitutional by a series of knowledgeable tutors. That, coupled with discussions on political matters with her father, and the influence of her grandmother, King George V's widow Queen Mary – whose stern aspect confirmed her view that royalty should not smile in public – fostered in her the keen sense of responsibility that has been her hallmark over 60 years. Respectful of her grandmother though she might be, the present Queen does smile. And when she does, as millions of her subjects all over the world have commented, 'her face lights up'.

PRINCE PHILIP

Prince Philip of Greece first met the elder daughter of King George VI at Dartmouth in 1939 when she was 13 and he was 18. He was a naval cadet, the son of Prince Andrew of Greece (seventh child of King George I of Greece and grandson of King Christian IX of Denmark) and Princess Alice of Battenburg – sister of Lord Louis Mountbatten. Like Elizabeth, Philip is a great, great-grandchild of Queen Victoria, and he and The Queen are third cousins. It is therefore not surprising that Philip was detailed to look after the two Princesses while The King and Queen were engaged on official business in Dartmouth, having arrived on board the Royal Yacht *Victoria and Albert*. It was, Elizabeth is reported to have said, "love at first sight" – for her at least.

Philip was born in 1921 on the island of Corfu at Mon Repos, a villa that was formerly the summer residence of the Greek king. Philip's family were exiled from Greece when he was 18 months old and moved to France. His earliest schooling took place in Paris – adding French to his existing vocabulary of English, German and Greek. But most of his young life was spent in the United Kingdom, at Cheam Preparatory School and then at Kurt Hahn's school, Gordonstoun, in Scotland. A brief spell at Hahn's school at Salem in Germany had been brought to a close by the rise of Nazism, when Philip's derisive hilarity at having to give the Nazi salute was an early indication of his future temperament. At one time sixth in line to the Greek throne, Philip renounced his title as Prince of Greece and Denmark in 1947 when he became a naturalized British subject. At the same time he took the anglicized form of his mother's maiden name, Mountbatten.

Elizabeth and Philip met for the second time in 1943 when Philip came to one of the pantomimes that the royal children put on each year at Windsor (that year it was *Aladdin*). He was on shore leave and sat in the front row. They began corresponding shortly afterwards, and Philip found himself invited more frequently to royal occasions. He spent Christmas with the family at Sandringham in 1943 and often visited Buckingham Palace in his MG sports car. (It was generally considered that he drove too fast.)

Prince Philip proposed to Princess Elizabeth in September 1946, but since his daughter was only 19, The King advised caution. Embarking with her family on a tour of South Africa would, thought The King, act as a 'cooling off period' – a test of their devotion. If Elizabeth should still be keen on marriage on her return, then he would give his blessing. She was and he did. Philip and Elizabeth became officially engaged on 10 July 1947 and were married at Westminster Abbey on 20 November 1947. Princess Elizabeth was 21 and her husband – dubbed Duke of Edinburgh by King George VI on the eve of his wedding – was 26.

The Princess, wearing her grandmother's tiara and a dress designed by Norman Hartnell, travelled to the Abbey in the Irish state coach with her father, in the uniform of an admiral of the fleet, sitting beside her. "It is a far more moving thing to give your daughter away than to be married yourself," The King told the Archbishop of York, Cyril Garbett, later that day. Two thousand people watched in the Abbey, a few saw the event when highlights were televised that evening (televisions were the province of a select few in 1947) and millions more around the world listened on the radio as the couple were married by the Archbishop of Canterbury, Dr Geoffrey Fisher.

Eight bridesmaids, two pages, along with a plentiful supply of royalty from other lands (some still in power, others deposed), members of both houses of parliament and a host of friends, dignitaries and other guests filled the Abbey with colour and sparkle. Long gowns and tiaras and uniforms dripping with braid only added to the spectacle that came as a welcome ray of sunshine just two years after the end of a long and wearying war.

After a wedding breakfast for 150 close friends at Buckingham Palace the couple were driven to Waterloo station in an open carriage – the princess now wearing a pale blue Hartnell creation described as 'love in a mist' – with a hot water bottle underneath the rug on her lap to keep her warm, along with her favourite corgi, Susan. From Waterloo they caught a train to Winchester.

The first night of their honeymoon was to be spent at Broadlands, the country home of the Mountbattens – Edwina and Philip's 'Uncle Dickie', Lord Mountbatten, near Romsey in Hampshire – something which would have delighted Mountbatten (a great-grandson of Queen Victoria), often accused of meddling in family matters and of actually lining up his nephew for marriage into the heart of the royal family. (Prince Philip's temperament suggests that it is unlikely he would have been made to do anything against his will, let alone marry for rank and position.)

The Duke and Duchess of Edinburgh's first home was Windlesham Moor, near Sunningdale, where they lived while Clarence House – named after the man who built it, William IV, formerly Duke of Clarence – was being renovated. Designed by John Nash and built between 1825 and 1827, the house was offered to the couple by The King. It is just a stone's throw from Buckingham Palace, on the eastern side of The Mall, a cheering thought to a man who would clearly relish having his daughter close by.

The King's first letter to the newly married Elizabeth will strike a chord with any father who has given his daughter away:

> I was so proud of you & thrilled at having you so close to me on our long walk in Westminster Abbey, but when I handed your hand to the Archbishop I felt I had lost something very precious.

The letter concludes:

> Your leaving us has left a great blank in our lives but do remember that your old home is still yours & do come back to it as much & as often as possible. I can see that

you are sublimely happy with Philip which is right but
don't forget us is the wish of
 Your ever loving & devoted
 Papa

THE CHILDREN

It was a moment of national rejoicing when Commander Richard Colville, RN, press secretary to His Majesty The King, walked across the courtyard of Buckingham Palace just after 11 p.m. on the evening of Sunday 14 November 1948 and fastened the following announcement, written in his own hand, to the railings:

Her Royal Highness the Princess Elizabeth, Duchess of Edinburgh, was safely delivered of a Prince at 9.14 o'clock this evening. Her Royal Highness and the infant Prince are both doing well.

The baby was delivered in the palace's Buhl Room (converted into a surgery with the best equipment that the age could muster). Prince Philip was informed of his first-born son's arrival while he was playing squash in the palace's court with his equerry. Outside a waiting crowd of several thousand greeted the arrival of the second in line to the throne with cheers and a spontaneous chorus of 'For he's a jolly good fellow'. Prince Philip raced to his wife's side with champagne and carnations. He was, said his equerry Mike Parker, "Over the moon. Absolutely delighted".

PRINCE CHARLES

Prince Charles Philip Arthur George – not to be created Prince of Wales until he was nine years old, and not to be formally invested with the title until 1969 – was born into a country still scarred by bomb damage and where many items of food were still rationed.

Charles was three years old when his mother became Queen and he sat between his grandmother and aunt at the coronation. Between the ages of five and eight he was educated at home by a governess – Catherine Peebles (Mispy), and then went on to Cheam and Gordonstoun (not especially happily), with a spell at Geelong Grammar School in Australia. He subsequently earned a Bachelor of Arts degree in Architecture and Anthropology from Trinity College, Cambridge, and spent a term at Aberystwyth studying Welsh and Welsh culture and history, while continuing to fit in his royal duties.

In the late 1940s and early 1950s, Britain was a nation where church membership was high, many children went to Sunday school, thrift and 'make do and mend' were the watch-words in most families, and great store was set by traditional values. People wanted to get married in church, women regarded it as the norm to be wives and mothers first and foremost, and two years' national service was compulsory for teenage boys. High moral standards pervaded personal and community life (in principle at least) and although class divisions were not as strong as they had been before the war, it was still possible to identify someone's social rank by their clothes and their accent. Broadcasters spoke 'received pronunciation' (what was commonly known as 'talking posh' – a bit like The Queen herself) and the nation was predominantly white; the first serious influx of immigrants from the West Indies occurred in 1947, but ten years later there were still only 36,000 resident in the United Kingdom.

At such a time, and in such circumstances, the lives of the monarch and her family were to some degree bound up with our own. The royals were, in effect, the first family, and one whose ancestry could be traced back to what ordinary folk regarded as the beginning of time. Their ancestry was our ancestry, and their history our history, in the days before the internet made genealogy popular and more readily explored. Even more importantly in those immediately post-war years, a king or a queen added sparkle to our lives, often quite literally by wearing a jewel-encrusted crown to open parliament, or simply dressing in gold-encrusted uniforms or ermine and pearls at state dinners and banquets, balls and ships' naming ceremonies. Trivial though it may seem, the royal family had the ability to make the lives of those they met or those who observed them just a touch more glamorous, and in the 1940s and 1950s Britain was sorely in need of a bit of glamour.

But Britain's people also knew that their King and Queen had seen them through the worst of times without shirking their duties, and with no apparent concern for their own safety. Along with Churchill they had pulled us through a harrowing world war, and while the former prime minister himself might be voted into opposition by a seemingly ungrateful country who wanted a different government once hostilities had ended, The King and Queen continued to be held in high esteem, as did their elder daughter and her husband, a man who – in spite of his rather confused ancestry (was he Greek, or Danish, or German?) – had served with distinction in the Royal Navy during the war (he was mentioned in despatches) and whose dashing good looks endeared him to most of the female population.

As a result, the arrival of a new Prince was celebrated all over the world. Ships were festooned with bunting, beacons were lit across the land, bells of churches and cathedrals rang peals and parliament congratulated the couple on the arrival of their first child who would, one day, be crowned King.

When the young Prince was barely a year old, his father, now aged 28, was appointed first lieutenant and second in command of HMS *Chequers*, the leader of the First Destroyer Flotilla in the Mediterranean Fleet in Malta. His wife went out to join him in Malta regularly, and although it meant leaving behind her young son for long periods of time, this period is referred to by many biographers as the time when – away from the glare of publicity – the couple could most be themselves, and lead as 'normal' a life as any royal ever could. Much of it was spent at the Villa Guardamangia, home of the Mountbattens (having relinquished his post as the last Viceroy of India, Mountbatten was now commander of the First Cruiser Squadron).

Throughout their lives Elizabeth and Philip would find themselves geographically distanced from all their children for varying periods of time – many of them far longer than any parent could wish for.

PRINCESS ANNE

What became clear was that whatever the logistical problems that their marriage might encounter, the couple were not content to settle for an only child. It was in Malta, during those often alluded to 'halcyon days' of their marriage, that The Prince's sister was conceived.

Princess Anne Elizabeth Alice Louise was born at Clarence House, where Elizabeth and Philip had now made their London home, at 11.50 a.m. on 15 August 1950. A robust and assertive child from the outset, Anne was destined for schooling at Benenden in Kent and to become one of the foremost horsewomen in the world. She was just two years old when her grandfather died, her father's promising naval career came to an abrupt end and her mother became Queen.

"THE KING IS DEAD, LONG LIVE THE QUEEN"

King George VI, in spite of a crippling lack of self-confidence, a tendency to temper tantrums known to the family as his 'gnashes', and a debilitating stammer, proved himself to be tenacious, dedicated and exactly the sort of king that was needed to lead his the country through World War II, with a wife at his side who became, more and more as the years passed, the darling of the nation in her large-brimmed hats and with her love of feathers and jewels. Queen Elizabeth, from her husband's accession in 1937 until her death in 2002 at the age of 101, seemed always at ease with her people, regardless of their status, and her popularity as the 'Queen Mum' seemed, at times, in danger of eclipsing that of her less demonstrative daughter.

Newspapers announced the death of King George VI and the nation mourned. Elizabeth flew back from Kenya to attend her father's funeral.

The King, never blessed with robust good health, and a lifelong smoker (he suffered from lung cancer), died of a heart attack at Sandringham on 6 February 1952, aged 56. Princess Elizabeth and her husband were on the first leg of a trip to Australia being undertaken on behalf of the ailing King. It was while they were at Sagana Lodge in Kenya – a gift from the Kenyan colonial government – that Elizabeth learned of her father's death. The news was broken to her by her husband, Prince Philip. When asked how she had taken it, The Prince replied: "Bravely, like a Queen."

DEATH OF QUEEN MARY

The Queen's grandmother lived long enough to see Queen Elizabeth II accede to the throne, but died on 24 March 1953, just three months before her beloved granddaughter's coronation. Her influence on the young Elizabeth had been profound, as had her role alongside King George V in modernizing the monarchy.

Immediately after the First World War the royal families of Europe were disappearing at an alarming rate – the most dramatic example being the assassination of the Russian royal family by Bolsheviks in 1917. King George V and Queen Mary – while more Victorian in their outlook than

The King's father, Edward VII – were nevertheless determined to make sure they fulfilled the needs of the nation, and made it their business to get out and about among their people more than ever before. The result was a modernization of the monarchy for which they are rarely credited.

On the death of King George VI, Prince Philip's uncle, Lord Louis Mountbatten, was keen for the family name to be changed from Windsor to Mountbatten – but Queen Mary was having none of it. King George V had changed the family name to Windsor from Saxe-Coburg-Gotha in 1917 and Queen Mary saw no reason why that should not continue. (In the event it was not until 1960 that a proclamation was made to the effect that future descendants of Queen Elizabeth II would bear the family name Mountbatten-Windsor, and its first recorded usage was by Princess Anne at her wedding in 1973.)

Throughout her life, the woman who had been born Princess Mary of Teck espoused a profound sense of loyalty to her country (her eldest son's abdication in 1936 caused her immense pain and anger). Invariably ram-rod straight and bedecked in a generous selection of pearl and diamond necklaces, Queen Mary instilled in her granddaughter a sense of duty which has never wavered. And there are moments when Queen Elizabeth II's facial expression owes more than a little to that of her paternal grandmother.

THE CORONATION

"At my coronation next June, I shall dedicate myself anew to your service. I shall do so in the presence of a great congregation, drawn from every part of the Commonwealth and Empire, while millions outside Westminster Abbey will hear the promises and prayers being offered up within its walls, and see much of the ancient ceremony in which kings and queens before me have taken part through century upon century.

"You will be keeping it as a holiday; but I want to ask you all, whatever your religion may be, to pray for me on that day – to pray that God may give me wisdom and strength to carry out the solemn promises I shall be making, and that I may faithfully serve Him and you all the days of my life."

THE QUEEN'S CHRISTMAS MESSAGE, 1952

The coronation of Queen Elizabeth II took place at Westminster Abbey on 2 June 1953 and represented the greatest national celebration since the end of the Second World War. Although legally and constitutionally The Queen became Queen the moment her father died, the ceremony of the coronation – the intertwining of church and state – is the most important and significant in any monarch's reign. The coronation represents the personal dedication of the monarch to the service of God and the people over whom the monarch reigns.

The coronation of Queen Elizabeth II took place 16 months after the death of her father. The delay between the death of one monarch and the coronation of the next is deliberate – not only to allow for the planning of such an elaborate ceremony, but also to allow for a full year of mourning. The month chosen was June – that being considered a time when good weather would be reasonably likely. It was not. It rained and the temperature managed to reach a mere 11°C.

And yet nothing could dampen the nation's spirits. The ceremony was organized by The Duke of Edinburgh and The Earl Marshall – The Duke of Norfolk – a stickler for protocol and an experienced handler of royal occasions. The ceremony itself was broadcast live on both radio and television all around the world in 44 different languages – an unprecedented number (for those times) – with 27 million watching on television (the first time cameras had been allowed to broadcast live from the Abbey).

Anyone who had a television was deluged by friends and neighbours anxious for a ringside seat, and the sale of television sets soared. For many it was the first thing they ever saw on television – and the broadcast lasted an astonishing 6 hours and 45 minutes.

The cabinet had advised against the televising of the coronation; the monarch overruled them, though the most deeply religious part of the ceremony – the anointing of the sovereign's head with oil – was not shown.

The prime minister, Winston Churchill, insisted that sweet rationing should end before the coronation so that everyone in the land might be able to celebrate with a bar of chocolate. On the morning of the coronation, in a gesture probably unrelated to this thoughtful consideration, The Queen made Churchill a Knight of the Garter. Lowlier mortals opted for simpler forms of decoration – painting their houses red, white and blue and organizing street parties that turned the nation into a day-long festival of national pride. And proud we were, of a serious-minded yet beautiful woman whose very existence promised to lead us out of wartime austerity into a new Elizabethan age.

A million out-of-towners descended on London to join the festivities, and a quarter of the world's population took the day off to celebrate.

Elizabeth II's coronation was the 28th to take place in Westminster Abbey and was conducted by the Archbishop of Canterbury in front of 7,500 peers, politicians and foreign dignitaries – many of them positioned on tiered ranks of seating especially constructed for the occasion. Foreign monarchs, by tradition, do not attend, sending instead the heirs to the throne. On this day the sovereign being crowned must be the highest-ranking presence.

At 11 a.m. the Gold State Coach – commonly known as the Golden Coach – left Buckingham Palace with The Queen inside. Built for King George III in 1762 and gilded with 24 carat gold, it weighs 24 tons and is pulled by eight Windsor Greys at a steady speed of 3 mph. It has been used for every coronation since that of King George IV, making The Queen the seventh sovereign to travel within its lavishly upholstered interior. Suspended upon leather straps, it is said to make the passengers feel a touch seasick.

As at her wedding almost six years earlier, The Queen was dressed by Norman Hartnell, this time in a gown of

Everyone was eager to be involved one way or another.

ILLUSTRATED—June 13, 1953

34

PERISCOPES GO U

For 130,000 of Her Majesty's subjects, TV is not enough. They had camped along the route all night, when the temperature went down to forty-four degrees. They had held their places against the millions who came in the morning. Thousands of them are at Marble Arch. As the Queen arrives they raise a forest of periscopes, scale a traffic light

T MARBLE ARCH

*The ever-unreliable British weather did nothing to weaken
the show of support for the popular young Queen.*

white satin, embroidered with symbols of England, Ireland, Scotland, Wales and the Commonwealth, and encrusted with gold and precious stones. Over her shoulders was draped a robe of crimson velvet – the same robe she wears today for the State Opening of Parliament – and upon her head the diamond and pearl circlet that is King George IV's State Diadem (dating from 1820 and still a prominent feature of our postage stamps).

Around her neck lay the diamond necklace of Queen Victoria, accompanied by matching earrings, and in her hands a bouquet of white flowers – lily-of-the-valley, orchids, stephanotis and carnations – all of them grown in the United Kingdom.

Six maids of honour preceded The Queen to the Abbey, ready to take charge of her long train as she stepped out of the golden coach and made her way down the long chancel to the throne. Traditionally the daughters of Dukes, Marquises and Earls, these six – Lady Mary Baillie-Hamilton, Lady Rosemary Spencer-Churchill, Lady Jane Vane-Tempest-Stewart, Lady Jane Heathcote-Drummond-Willoughby, Lady Anne Coke and Lady Moyra Hamilton – still recall with crystal clarity their feelings on that day and how astonished they were at The Queen's composure. They were equally astonished at having been chosen for the role, most of them having had little previous contact with their new sovereign. "We were," says Lady

Anne Coke (now The Rt Hon The Lady Glenconner), "the Spice Girls of our day. There was quite a lot of jealousy among those who had not been chosen."

The maids of honour had rehearsed their role at the palace with The Queen and a long sheet. Such is their memory, though Ede and Ravenscroft, the royal robe makers, were commissioned to make a 'mock robe' for the princely (if not queenly) sum of £9. The Queen was not part of the Abbey rehearsals; only on the day did the maids of honour experience the true weight of the occasion, and of the long robe, and only one of them needed the smelling salts that were concealed in their gloves on the advice of The Duke of Norfolk.

The Queen's arrival was heralded with a fanfare of trumpets, and from the West Door, where she was met by The Duke of Norfolk, she took her place in the procession of church dignitaries and other important personages, standard bearers, Knights of the Garter, prime ministers of the UK and Commonwealth, preceded by peers carrying the royal regalia – a priceless collection of crown jewels dating from the reign of King Charles II (newly minted after the depredations of Cromwell and the Civil War) and consisting of swords, sceptres, spurs and an orb. Two new gold armills (coronation bracelets) were made especially for The Queen's coronation, and along with these symbols of regal power were borne the Bible, the chalice and the paten –

CORONATION OF HER MAJESTY
QUEEN ELIZABETH II

By Command of The Queen

the Earl Marshal is directed to invite

to be present at the Abbey Church of
Westminster on the 2nd day of June 1953

Norfolk.
Earl Marshal

*A crowd of thousands attended the coronation,
the 28th to take place in Westminster Abbey.*

the whole procession symbolizing the joining together of church and state.

"Vivat Regina Elizabetha," sang the scholars of Westminster School, as The Queen entered, and the elaborate ceremony began; divided into five parts – the recognition, the oath, the anointing with holy oil, the investiture and the crowning, when the magnificent St Edward's Crown of 1661 is held above the sovereign's head and lowered into place as the assembled congregation shouts "God Save The Queen!" and the trumpets are sounded. Outside at the

Tower of London and in Hyde Park guns are fired in cere-monial salute.

The Queen was then blessed and enthroned, and at this point the key personages swore allegiance to Her Majesty, among them the Archbishop of Canterbury and The Duke of Edinburgh, bowing before her and kissing her on the left cheek.

"God save Queen Elizabeth! Long live Queen Eliz-abeth! May The Queen live for ever!" Shouted or sung to the music of 'Zadok the Priest' by Handel, the words rang out several times during the coronation ceremony, and after taking Holy Communion, The Queen repaired to St Edward's Chapel where a purple velvet coronation robe was substituted for the crimson Robe Royal, and the heavy St Edward's Crown (at 2.23 kg (4 lbs 9 oz)) was replaced by the Imperial State Crown of 1937 (used for the State Opening of Parliament and slightly lighter at around 900 g (2lb)).

The Queen then made her way in procession to the West Door and embarked upon her journey back to Buckingham Palace in the state coach, this time using a longer route of five miles that would take 1 hour and 40 minutes so that as many people as possible would get to see her. (So long was the procession, and so great the number of coaches that were needed, that several had to be hired from a film company!) Queen Salote of Tonga famously defied the weather and left the top of her coach down so that the crowds could see her. "Who is the small man sitting next to her?" someone asked Noël Coward. "Her lunch," he replied.

For those who witnessed it, the coronation was an event never to be forgotten. Whether viewed by those privileged to have a seat in the Abbey, in front of a television, or from a London street corner, stories still abound of the day when grey skies and persistent drizzle could do nothing to dampen the enthusiasm of a nation about to embark on a new life.

The day after the coronation, news reached British shores that the New Zealander Edmund Hillary had become the first man to conquer Mount Everest – the highest mountain in the world at 8,848 m (29,028 feet). He had achieved the hitherto dreamed-of feat the day before The Queen had been crowned. It seemed like a happy omen.

THE RISE OF TELEVISION

1950   There were only 344,000 television sets in Britain.

1951   The number of television sets had doubled.

1953   There was a rush to buy television sets for the
        coronation, but there was still only one channel: BBC.

1955 ITV began transmitting.

The first advert was broadcast: for Gibbs SR toothpaste.

1957 Radio audiences dropped as 6 million people were now watching BBC and ITV nightly.

The first television detector vans came into use, prosecuting those who did not have a licence.

Teenage programmes started – with 'live' audiences: Six-Five Special on BBC.

1958 The State Opening of Parliament was televised for the first time.

1959 There were 24.5 million television sets in Britain: two-thirds of adults owned what became popularly known as a 'gogglebox'.

People watched an average of 12 hours of television a week. Seven and a half million could still only receive BBC, not ITV.

Cinema audiences slumped.

THE 1950s

"So this will be a voyage right round the world – the first that a Queen of England has been privileged to make as Queen. But what is really important to me is that I set out on this journey in order to see as much as possible of the people and countries of the Commonwealth and Empire, to learn at first hand something of their triumphs and difficulties, and something of their hopes and fears."

THE QUEEN'S CHRISTMAS MESSAGE, 1953

On her accession to the throne, The Queen and Prince Philip moved into Buckingham Palace and inherited new living quarters in the form of Windsor Castle, Sandringham and Balmoral – the last two being the sovereign's private family residences. King George VI's widow, from now on to be known as 'Queen Elizabeth The Queen Mother', moved with her daughter Princess Margaret into Clarence House, where she was to remain for the rest of her life. (To this day in royal circles she is known as 'Queen Elizabeth', her daughter being referred to as 'The Queen'.)

It was in 1952 that The Queen Mother bought Barrogill Castle in Caithness, on the north coast of Scotland, giving it back its old name of The Castle of Mey. At that time it was little more than a ruin, but The Queen Mother set about restoring it, and would holiday there each August until shortly before her death in 2002. Since then The Duke of Rothesay (Prince Charles's Scottish title) has taken it under his wing and continues to visit it himself and to ensure its upkeep via the Friends of The Castle of Mey.

IN THE 1950s

(Prices have been converted into decimal currency)

Prime ministers	Winston Churchill (1951–5); Anthony Eden (1955–7); Harold Macmillan (1957–63)
Price of a pint of milk	1.9p
Price of a loaf of bread	1.9p
Price of a dozen eggs	8.8p
Price of petrol	22.5p per gallon; 5p per litre
Average weekly wage	£10
Average house price	£2,000
On TV	Dixon of Dock Green; Tonight; Hancock's Half Hour; What's My Line?

TOUR OF THE COMMONWEALTH

Originally planned to be undertaken by her father, The Queen's tour of the Commonwealth lasted from November 1953 to May 1954 and covered a total of 70,196 km

(43,618 miles). A tour of such length and duration would be unthinkable nowadays. The longest of The Queen's trips is measured in weeks, not months, and the speed and efficiency of air travel has made such long absences unnecessary. Bermuda, Jamaica, Panama and Fiji were visited, and in Tonga The Queen and Duke were ferried around in the London taxi that Queen Salote had taken back with her after the coronation. There were banquets and balls, luncheons, dinners and innumerable loyal toasts – the sort of things that most ordinary folk would find wearying in the extreme. To The Queen and The Duke they are a part of daily life; the royal ritual.

The Queen reached New Zealand in time for Christmas, and her Christmas message of 1953 was broadcast live from Government House in Auckland. While they were there, a loyal sheep farmer dyed his flock red, white and blue and displayed them so that his expression of loyalty could be viewed clearly from the windows of the royal train.

The tour continued throughout 1954 with visits to Australia, the Cocos Islands, Ceylon (Sri Lanka), Aden, Uganda, Gibraltar, Libya and Malta.

All this time The Queen's children – Prince Charles and Princess Anne, now aged five and three – remained at home in London in the care of their grandmother.

It shocks and horrifies many people today that The Queen and Duke left behind such young children to embark on such a lengthy tour. But The Queen and Duke were no ordinary parents: as Head of the Commonwealth it was The Queen's duty to visit foreign lands; her responsibility to her children was but one part of her life; the other – and it was a large and an important one – was to her people. It should also be remembered that back in the 1950s, particularly among the upper classes, leaving one's children behind to be looked after by grandparents was not nearly so frowned upon as it sometimes is today. For forces' families it was a way of life, and many children of well-off parents were sent away to boarding school from the age of four or five. At least the young Prince and Princess were in the care of nurses they liked and a grandmother they adored; a grandmother whose own sense of duty – "Your devoir" as she called it all her life – was highly developed. Prince Philip's concern was less about parental absence than that the children would be spoiled by their indulgent grandmother!

Often referred to as a mother who was not overly demonstrative in terms of affection expressed towards her children, the burden of state upon The Queen's shoulders would certainly have compromised the amount of time she could spend with her offspring on a daily basis, but The Princess Royal recalls happy memories of parents who could chase after them in family games much faster than they could run themselves, and of a father whose bedtime stories

*A delicate balancing act – although the duty expected
of The Queen by her people was a heavy burden, the
role required by her family was still important.*

were second to none – hardly the memories of a uniformly
unhappy or deprived childhood.

Did The Queen miss her children on these extended
visits? Undoubtedly. She also missed her husband, whose
own three-month tour of the southern hemisphere in 1956
on board HMY *Britannia* – visiting Ceylon, Malaya, Australia, New Zealand, Antarctica and the Falklands – gave rise
to much speculation on the state of their young marriage.
In her Christmas message of that year she said: "You will
understand me, therefore, when I tell you that of all the
voices we have heard this afternoon none has given my children and myself greater joy than that of my husband. To
him I say: 'From all the members gathered here today our
very best good wishes go out to you and everyone on board

Britannia as you voyage together in the far southern seas. Happy Christmas from us all.'"

Measured, yes; but heartfelt nonetheless. The trip had been undertaken partially as sea trials for the newly launched royal yacht, but some felt that it was a clear sign of a marital rift. The concerns were groundless. Sixty-four years on, the couple has one of the most enduring and admired marriages.

"It is inevitable that I should seem a rather remote figure to many of you. A successor to the kings and queens of history; someone who may be familiar in newspapers and films but who never really touches your personal lives. But now at least for a few minutes I welcome you into the peace of my own home."

THE QUEEN'S CHRISTMAS MESSAGE, 1957

THE CONSORT

On The Queen's accession to the throne Prince Philip gave up his naval career "just when it was getting interesting". He has not, up to the time of writing, been granted the official title of 'Prince Consort' as bestowed upon Prince

Albert by a devoted Queen Victoria. It is suggested that he does not seek it. What is certain is that he has fulfilled the role in all but name. Neither has he complained about 'the job' and the fact that it has deprived him of what would almost certainly have been a high-powered naval career.

The word duty comes to the fore again. Try to talk to The Duke about personal achievements and you will discover, to your cost, that he is not the slightest bit interested in blowing his own trumpet. His duty – almost his very existence – is to support The Queen. Suggest that his own achievements are worthy of praise and he will prevaricate or deny. The Duke of Edinburgh's Award? "Kurt Hahn's idea." Actively serving in the war? "So did everybody else." His attitude is interpreted by many as arrogance. Bearing in mind the pattern of his life thus far, a touch of arrogance would seem to be implicit in his character. But I firmly believe that a greater part of The Prince's attitude towards those who seek to explore his own achievements is a genuine dislike of putting himself before The Queen. Only when talking about interests such as carriage driving and nature will The Prince open up with a marked degree of enthusiasm. It says much about his character and the way he has carried himself over the last 60 years.

The Prince accompanies The Queen on all her Commonwealth tours and state visits. He is patron of around 800 organizations and although at the age of 90, and after a heart attack in 2011, he is beginning to relinquish some patronages and presidencies in favour of younger members of the family, he says he is, according to The Princess Royal, going through his 'Still phase' – the phase during which people ask him "Are you *still* there?"

On the royal estates he has a passion for planting avenues of trees; his work in making the estates more efficient has had far-reaching results in terms of economy and technology; he designs barbecues and trailers to carry equipment; he uses his own London taxi to get around town and dislikes comments on his standard of driving, even threatening to put The Queen out when they drive around the Crown Estate if she complains of his driving too fast. When a friend suggested that this course of action was, in reality, unlikely, The Queen replied forcefully, "He would!"

He is, however, a man of apparent contradictions. Famously hostile to the press, it was he who encouraged The Queen to allow Richard Cawston's controversial film, *Royal Family*, to go ahead in 1969. He was the first president of the World Wildlife Fund at its inception in 1961 and continues as President Emeritus of its successor, the World Wide Fund for Nature (WWF); he also shoots game.

He has his own annual Designer's Prize – established in 1959 – with Sir James Dyson and Sir Terence Conran among the notable recipients (1997 and 2003 respectively). He is chancellor of a number of universities, Admiral of the Royal

Yacht Squadron, patron of the Grand Order of Water Rats and of the Hastings Winkle Club. Until age and arthritis got the better of him he was a fearsome polo player. He then turned to carriage driving, a sport at which he excels (though no longer competitively), and played a major part in writing the rulebook for the sport. He has successfully competed in national and international sailing competitions in his yachts *Coweslip* and *Bluebottle* and launched (at the suggestion of Kurt Hahn, of course) The Duke of Edinburgh's Award Scheme. Since its inception in 1959 the scheme has been participated in by over six million young people in more than 60 countries. He still puts in an appearance at the Gold Award ceremonies (Gold Awards are not lightly won) and has a great capacity to make young folk laugh.

PRINCE PHILIP AND PAINTING

As well as collecting art from time to time, Prince Philip has also painted in oils since the early days of his marriage. The East Anglian artist Edward Seago accompanied The Prince on his voyage aboard *Britannia* in 1956 and the two painted together. When asked if Seago was a good teacher The Prince replied, "Hopeless," though his own style clearly owes something to his sometime mentor. He told me he judges his own canvases not by their artistic merit, but by whether or not he enjoyed producing them.

PRINCE PHILIP'S TITLES AND HONOURS

His Royal Highness The Prince Philip, Duke of Edinburgh, Earl of Merioneth and Baron Greenwich, KG (Knight of the Garter), KT (Knight of the Thistle), OM (Order of Merit), GBE (Knight Grand Cross of the Most Excellent Order of the British Empire), AC (Companion of the Order of Australia), QSO (Companion of The Queen's Service Order), PC (Privy Counsellor)

1947   Knight of the Order of the Garter

1952   Knight of the Order of the Thistle

1953   Grand Master of the Order of the British Empire

1957   The Queen conferred upon Prince Philip 'the style and dignity of a Prince of the United Kingdom'

1968   Appointed to the Order of Merit

2011   Appointed Lord High Admiral by The Queen

HER MAJESTY'S YACHT *BRITANNIA*

By 1950 the Royal Yacht *Victoria and Albert III* was 50 years old and was at the end of her useful life. Her replacement, HMY *Britannia*, steamed out to meet The Queen and Prince Philip in Tobruk, Libya, at the end of their 1953 Commonwealth tour. It carried the young Prince Charles and Princess Anne to meet their parents at the end of that long separation.

Victoria and Albert III cost £572,000; *Britannia* cost £2 million, and Prince Philip, no doubt relishing the prospect of being involved with shipping once more, was involved in her design and fit-out – the latter with the assistance of Sir Hugh Casson.

Unusually for a ship, *Britannia* carried her name neither on her bow nor her stern yet she remained one of the most recognizable ships afloat. Unostentatious in design, her hull is a glistening blue–black and a gold stripe runs around the topside of her hull. She became the family's home away from home – the place where they could relax, away from the prying eyes of the world's press. (Signals between the crew were famously given by hand to minimize disturbance, and soft deck shoes were worn to avoid unnecessary noise.)

The United Kingdom's 83rd Royal Yacht (King Charles II had the first), until her decommissioning in December

⟡HMY *BRITANNIA*: FACTS AND FIGURES ⟡

Launched by	HM The Queen on 16 April 1953 at John Brown's Clydebank shipyard
Length overall	125.65 m (412 ft 3 in)
Beam	16.7 m (55 ft)
Draft	5.2 m (15 ft 7 in)
Gross tonnage	5,862 tons
Maximum speed	22.5 knots
Engines	two geared steam turbines developing a total of 12,000 shaft horsepower
Range	2,553 miles at 18 knots
Propeller diameter	3.12 m (10 ft 3 in)

1997, HMY *Britannia* made 968 official voyages, travelled 1,087,623 nautical miles and visited 600 ports in 135 countries.

Though modestly furnished by royal standards, the yacht became a floating palace where The Queen and Duke could entertain foreign heads of state around the world, and many royal couples spent all or part of their honeymoon on board.

When not in use by the royal family the ship became a floating ambassador for Britain and an effective venue for promoting British trade. Her 'Sea Days', whereby prominent international business figures came aboard to discuss commercial opportunities, resulted in countless business deals and exports – something overlooked by a government concerned that after 44 years of service a refit would prove too costly and that the public had no appetite to recommission a new vessel.

Prince Philip believes this to have been a great mistake, saying that *Britannia* was "sound as a bell" and given new diesel turbines would have had many more years of life ahead of her as a Royal Yacht – and a valuable resource for British trade.

HMY *Britannia*'s decommissioning in Portsmouth on 11 December 1997 was one of those all too rare occasions when The Queen was seen to wipe a tear from her eye. In a country famed for its seafaring history, she was not the only one.

THE COMMONWEALTH

The Commonwealth, which celebrated its 60th anniversary in 2009, has its origins in Queen Victoria's great British Empire.

The Queen does not rule it, but has the same role as she has with government – to consult, to advise and to warn. Having been at its head for 60 years, she is revered by foreign heads of state and her experience of global affairs is second to none.

The Commonwealth comprises 53 independent countries with historic links to Britain. They were all either ruled or administered by Britain or another member of the Commonwealth and accept The Queen as their titular head. English is spoken in all member countries, but not necessarily as the first language. In practice the Commonwealth is used as a trading area and the member countries have many unofficial links through culture, professions and sports – the Commonwealth games are held every four years. A Commonwealth service, attended by The Queen, is held in Westminster Abbey each March as part of the Commonwealth Day celebrations.

The Queen is head of state of 15 Commonwealth realms in addition to the UK, and the heads of these realms together with those of the independent member republics meet every two years at the Commonwealth Summit. It is at this summit that The Queen has the opportunity to meet all the Commonwealth leaders individually.

A country can withdraw from the Commonwealth at any time, as did the Republic of Ireland in 1949 and Zimbabwe in 2003, and it can also be expelled, as happened with South Africa in the 1960s (readmitted in the 1990s).

Nigeria, Fiji and Pakistan have been suspended more recently, and then readmitted.

OVERSEAS TERRITORIES

These are territories belonging by settlement, conquest or annexation to the British, Australian or New Zealand Crown. In such territories The Queen is represented by governors or commissioners. The UK Government is responsible for the security of the overseas territories and for foreign affairs and defence matters, but most territories have their own government. The British overseas territories are: British Indian Ocean Territory; Gibraltar; Bermuda; the Falkland Islands; South Georgia and the South Sandwich Islands; British Antarctic Territory; St Helena and its dependencies (Ascension and Tristan da Cunha); Montserrat; the British Virgin Islands; the Cayman Islands; the Turks and Caicos Islands; Anguilla; the Pitcairn Group of Islands; and the Sovereign base areas on Cyprus.

There are seven Australian external territories, two New Zealand dependent territories and two New Zealand associated states.

Hong Kong, a former overseas territory, held by Britain on a long lease, was handed back to China on 1 July 1997 in a ceremony attended by HRH The Prince of Wales and the last Governor, Chris Patten.

Crises occur from time to time, as they did with Rhodesia in 1979 when Prime Minister Ian Smith made a unilateral declaration of independence, illegally severing its links with the British Crown. After much fighting between minority whites and black guerrillas and the imposition of sanctions, the Commonwealth Summit in Lusaka played its part in calming things down. The end result was, indeed, independence in 1980, but under a different leader, Robert Mugabe, and a different name – Zimbabwe.

In Canada in the late 1970s Prime Minister Pierre Trudeau proposed ending Britain's constitutional role in the country but a compromise was reached. As a result, The Queen remains their titular head but without constitutional authority.

Throughout the 1980s Britain's relations with South Africa were strained and sanctions proposed as a protest against apartheid. Eventually the Commonwealth played its part in ending apartheid and Nelson Mandela was released on 11 February 1990 after 27 years in prison. He went on to become the president of South Africa in 1994.

THE QUEEN'S FAITH

Implicit in everything The Queen does – and frequently at the heart of her Christmas message – is her strong belief in God. Every Sunday, wherever she is in the world, The

Queen goes to church, though she takes Holy Communion only a handful of times a year. She was confirmed in March 1942, with her sister Margaret, by Archbishop Lang in St George's Chapel, Windsor. When staying at Windsor she will worship in the chapel; at Sandringham it will be the church of St Mary Magdalene, and at Balmoral, Crathie Kirk. The routine is unfailing, and while church attendance continues to fall across the country, The Queen remains an active 'defender of the faith'.

THE DETRACTORS

It would be both foolish and inaccurate to claim that the monarchy has been wholeheartedly admired by every member of its sovereign nation. Over the years there have been a number of vociferous detractors, and the criticism began early. Playwright John Osborne, the original 'angry young man', wrote in 1957: "My objection to the royal symbol is that it is dead; it is the gold filling in a mouthful of decay." He went on: "When the mobs rush forward in The Mall they are taking part in a last circus of a civilization that has lost faith in itself and sold itself for a splendid triviality."

Labour cabinet minister Richard Crossman observed the way he and his cabinet colleagues behaved in the presence of royalty, remarking that he, Barbara Castle and Roy

Jenkins found the whole thing uncomfortable, whereas George Brown, Fred Peart, Jim Callaghan and Harold Wilson were much more at ease: "... roughly speaking, it is true that it is the professional classes who in this sense are radical and the working-class socialists who are by and large staunchly monarchist. The nearer The Queen they get the more the working-class members of cabinet love her and she loves them ..."

And that, it seems, is still the case today. Time and again the so-called 'chattering classes' – self-styled arbiters of social wisdom – underestimate the affection in which the Crown is held by the vast majority of the public. The case is proven by events such as Queen Elizabeth's Lying in State, which had to be extended, so large were the numbers of people who wanted to pay their respects. The same has been true of The Queen's 80th birthday and the Golden Jubilee – both hugely popular. Alas, the 'chattering classes' are often possessed of that least attractive of attributes, mean-spiritedness. It is not, mercifully, an affliction of the majority of folk, which these royal occasions tend to prove.

THE SUEZ CRISIS

Just four years after her accession and three years after the coronation, the Suez Crisis rocked the nation. President

Nasser of Egypt threatened to nationalize the Suez Canal – the link between the Mediterranean and the Red Sea. Since the turn of the century the Canal had been under the protection of the British, until 1954 when the troops were finally withdrawn with an agreement from Nasser that the Canal would not be nationalized. In January 1956 Britain and the USA pledged to help fund a proposed new dam at Aswan, but increased Soviet influence over Egypt and Nasser's purchase of Soviet arms led to the funding later being withdrawn. In July 1956 Nasser moved to nationalize the Canal and the upshot was the invasion of Egypt by Israel on 29 October 1956, followed a day later by the British and French issuing an ultimatum to both Israel and Egypt to stop the fighting and then bombing Cairo. Both the USA and Russia were highly disapproving and accusations of collusion between France, Britain and Israel – though denied – were rife. President Dwight D. Eisenhower – 'Ike' – made the USA's loan of funds to Britain, to shore up sterling and prevent the pound being devalued, conditional upon a ceasefire. By the end of the year British and French troops had been withdrawn, though the Israelis remained until the following March. By April the Canal was once more open to all shipping. The whole affair brought about the end of the already ailing Prime Minister Anthony Eden's career; he resigned in January 1957.

THE QUEEN AND TELEVISION

The Queen's sixth Christmas broadcast in 1957 was ground-breaking in that it was the first to be televised; it was also the 25th anniversary of the first Christmas broadcast on 'the wireless' made by The Queen's grandfather, King George V. The 1957 broadcast was made from the long library at Sandringham.

The following year's message reflected the ramifications of such 'opening up' when, in her 1958 Christmas broadcast, The Queen acknowledges the fact that many people had written in, anxious to see the royal children on screen. At this time Prince Charles and Princess Anne would have been aged ten and eight respectively. The Queen was cautious, saying in her 1958 broadcast: "We value your interest in them and I can assure you we have thought about this a great deal before deciding against it. We would like our son and daughter to grow up as normally as possible so that they will be able to serve you and the Commonwealth faithfully and well when they are old enough to do so. We believe that public life is not a fair burden to place on growing children. I am sure that all of you who are parents will understand."

Ten years later, all that would change.

THIS THING CALLED TECHNOLOGY

After years of wartime stagnation, things were beginning to move forward. From now on we would enter the technological revolution – slowly at first, but then faster and faster until we just never knew how we managed before.

1952   The London tram goes out of service.

Britain launches the world's first passenger jet airliner, the De Havilland Comet.

Britain explodes its first nuclear bomb on an island north of Australia.

1953   Car prices plummet. A Ford Popular costs £390; an Austin A30 £475.

BOAC (The British Overseas Airways Corporation) has seven Comet aircraft in service around the world.

1954   Flashing indicator lights on cars are now a legal requirement.

1955   A motorway network is planned.

1956   The first electric railway services are to replace steam trains.

Third class rail travel is abolished.

The Queen opens the world's first commercial nuclear

power station at Calder Hall. (It closed in 2003 after 47 years in commission.)

1957 There is a plutonium scare in milk after a radioactivity leak from Windscale atomic works in Cumberland. Prime Minister Harold Macmillan tells the nation: "You've never had it so good!" (The two events not connected ...)

1958 The Hovercraft was invented by Christopher Cockerell.

Parking meters are trialled in Mayfair and the first yellow lines are introduced in London.

LP records, playing at 33 rpm, are now in production.

Bubble cars go on display at the Motor Show.

British Comet aircraft begin transatlantic service to New York.

The first stretch of motorway opens with the 8-mile Preston bypass in Lancashire.

The drug thalidomide is launched in Britain by the Distillers Company as a cure for morning sickness in pregnant women. It would be 1961 before the drug was withdrawn, having damaged 10,000 babies worldwide. Of the 2,000 born in Britain – with deformed or absent limbs – only 466 survived.

1959   The M1 opens, running from just north of Watford to the Midlands.

The BMC Mini is produced, costing £500.

Duty-free booze perk starts for air travellers.

The first postcodes are introduced.

THE QUEEN'S HOMES

BUCKINGHAM PALACE

Regarded today as the hub of the monarchy, Buckingham Palace began its life as the home of Lord Arlington in 1677 and subsequently of The Duke of Buckingham. King George III bought Buckingham House in 1762 as a private family residence for his wife Queen Charlotte, as distinct from their official residence at St James's Palace. Fourteen of the King's 15 children were born here.

Extended by George III, and subsequently by George IV who enlisted the architect John Nash to make considerable additions, the building became the monarch's principal residence from the time of Queen Victoria onwards (her predecessor William IV never lived here). Further work was undertaken by the architect Edward Blore in the 1830s, and Thomas Cubitt was responsible for the east wing – the 'front' of the palace – built in 1846–50. In 1913 it was refaced in Portland Stone to replace the inferior Caen stone, which was weathering badly. The palace, situated at the end of The Mall, has 775 rooms, 4.82 km (3 miles) of corridors and today employs 800 members of staff inside and out. The principal State Rooms are contained in the west wing (at the 'back') which overlooks the palace gardens. The private apartments of The Queen and The Duke, The Princess Royal and The Duke of York are in the north and east wings.

The ground floor of the palace consists mainly of offices, the State Rooms being on the first floor. These elegant and lofty chambers are wonderfully spectacular, with gilded pillars and pilasters and a fine collection of mainly Regency furniture. The White Drawing Room, the Music Room (where several royal christenings have taken place) and the Blue Drawing Room are the principal reception rooms, all of them opening on to the long Picture Gallery, which contains a priceless collection of Old Masters. The Ballroom is where investitures and banquets are held. During the course of the year some 50,000 people will visit the palace as guests, whether at banquets or investitures (occasions at which honours are awarded), lunches, dinners, receptions and Royal Garden Parties. Because Buckingham Palace is a working palace, it remains closed to the public for most of the year; however, the 19 State Rooms are opened to visitors in August and September when The Queen travels to Balmoral.

The Centre Room is on the first floor of the east wing and opens on to the balcony on which the royal family appears at Trooping the Colour and royal weddings. The decorations in this room are in the Chinese style.

The Royal Standard flies from the flagpole on top of the palace when The Queen is in residence. When she is not the Union flag is flown (an innovation since the death of The Princess of Wales when public demand for a flag to be flown at half mast resulted in its appearance). Every morning at 9 a.m. sharp The Queen's piper plays beneath her windows.

The palace sits in 40 acres of grounds, which include a 4-acre lake. Its garden boasts a fine collection of trees and shrubs, among which visitors can stroll at Royal Garden Parties. The grounds continue to be developed over the years and include a 175-yard long herbaceous border and a rose garden. In 1961 The Queen and The Duke added a curved avenue of Indian horse chestnut trees.

Buckingham Palace today is very much the HQ from which the monarchy is run, and seen by The Queen as 'the office'. When in London she is in residence there from Monday through to Friday, when she moves to Windsor Castle.

WINDSOR CASTLE

The largest occupied castle in the world – with around 1,000 rooms – Windsor Castle was originally built by William the Conqueror, out of wood. Many monarchs have subsequently added to the castle whose image is very much a national icon.

Used by The Queen as her weekend home, the castle has been utilized more and more recently for formal duties, including investitures. In addition The Queen resides here for a month in March and April, known as the Easter Court, and for a week in June when the Order of the Garter ceremony and Royal Ascot take place. State visits and banquets are also hosted in the castle.

The castle is situated in Windsor Great Park, a 5,000-acre deer park 20 miles from London, which was established in the thirteenth century. The Duke of Edinburgh is the Ranger of the Great Park, overseeing its maintenance and protection, and he has been responsible for much of the tree planting over the last 60 years. His interest is active and ongoing.

St George's Chapel, attached to the castle, is a Royal Peculiar – it is not subject to the jurisdiction of a bishop or archbishop but owes its allegiance directly to the sovereign. The wedding of Prince Edward and Sophie Rhys-Jones took place here in 1999, as did the service of dedication and prayer after the marriage of The Prince of Wales and The Duchess of Cornwall in 2005.

Queen Elizabeth The Queen Mother is buried in the chapel here with her husband King George VI.

Several parts of the castle are open to the public, and the Royal Archives and the Royal Photographic Collection are based here. Many of the drawings, photos and artefacts from these collections are displayed in changing exhibitions throughout the year.

ROYAL LODGE, WINDSOR

Just 3 miles south of Windsor Castle, Royal Lodge was just a small cottage in the seventeenth century until it was converted into a cottage orné by John Nash for The Prince Regent, who moved in in 1815. The Queen lived at Royal Lodge with her parents before her father acceded to the throne, and it was the residence of The Queen Mother after the death of King George VI. It is now home to The Duke of York. In its grounds is the miniature cottage 'Y Bwthyn Bach', given to Princess Elizabeth in 1932 by the people of Wales.

THE PALACE OF HOLYROODHOUSE

The Queen's official Edinburgh residence, Holyroodhouse was used by Queen Victoria as a stopping-off point en route to Balmoral. The present Queen spends two weeks here each July undertaking official engagements, including the Scottish garden parties.

Completed by King James V and added to by subsequent monarchs, the palace sits at the end of the Royal Mile, leading to Edinburgh Castle. It was originally a religious house founded in the twelfth century by King David I of Scotland and takes its name from a fragment of the holy rood (the cross), which resided here. Mary Queen of Scots spent much of her eventful life at Holyroodhouse. The palace and grounds are open to the public when The Queen is not in residence.

BALMORAL CASTLE

The sovereign's private Scottish home was acquired and rebuilt by Queen Victoria and Prince Albert in the nineteenth century. Originally a fifteenth-century castle, it sits on the banks of the River Dee in Aberdeenshire. The 'new' castle, built of Scottish granite, was completed in 1855 and the previous one demolished in 1856. It is not an official residence – owned by the state – but belongs to The Queen and her family. This is where The Queen and Duke retreat to for their summer holidays in August, September and early October. They come to hunt, shoot and fish, and to enjoy long walks and picnics. Originally the castle sat in

*Balmoral offers withdrawal from the public eye, and is where the royal
family have been known to return in times of crisis or mourning.*

11,000 acres but this has been extended over the years and
today stands at around 50,000 acres. Here, as in Windsor
Great Park, The Duke takes an active role in tree planting
and land management in the challenging terrain of moor-
land and Scottish woodland.

BIRKHALL

Situated on the Balmoral Estate, on the River Muick just
outside Ballater, Birkhall was acquired by Prince Albert in
1849. Built in 1715, the house was extensively refurbished

by The Queen Mother after the death of King George VI and she used it as her Scottish home. It is now the Scottish residence of The Prince of Wales and The Duchess of Cornwall who, when they are in Scotland, use the titles of The Duke and Duchess of Rothesay. Fishing, walking and gardening are the favourite pursuits at Birkhall.

SANDRINGHAM HOUSE

Another private residence, Sandringham House was acquired by Queen Victoria for her son, The Prince of Wales (the future King Edward VII) in 1862. She hoped it would be a healthy retreat, far enough away from the distractions of the city to allow her 'wayward' son to concentrate his mind on other things. Alas, the invention of the internal combustion engine made access to the city much easier. Prince Albert, who had begun the search for his son's house, died of typhoid fever in 1861, and so it was left to The Prince of Wales himself to settle on Sandringham, which became a home to him and his new bride, Princess Alexandra of Denmark, after their marriage in 1863.

The house was subsequently completely rebuilt to accommodate a growing family and larger social events and the 20,000-acre estate provided ample opportunities for The Prince to indulge his passion for shooting. So keen was The Prince on his sport that the clocks in the house were permanently set on 'Sandringham Time' – half an hour fast, so that as much time as possible could be spent outdoors in winter (a tradition that continued until it was abolished by King Edward VIII in 1936).

It was at Sandringham that King George V died in 1936 – in the home from which he had made the very first live royal broadcast to the nation in 1932. The present Queen made her first televised royal broadcast from Sandringham on Christmas Day 1957. Lady Diana Spencer, one day to be Princess of Wales, was born at Park House on the Sandringham estate in 1961.

The house was first visited by Queen Elizabeth II in 1926, aged just eight months, and today she spends Christmas and the New Year here with her family in the peace and quiet of the Norfolk countryside. When she and other members of the royal family are not in residence the house is open to the public, and the Sandringham Flower Show, held in July each year, is well worth a visit.

THE 1960s

"Mankind continues to achieve wonders in technical and space research but in the western world perhaps the launching of Telstar has captured the imagination most vividly. This tiny satellite has become the invisible focus of a million eyes. Telstar, and her sister satellites as they arise, can now show the world to the world just as it is in its daily life. What a wonderfully exciting prospect and perhaps it will make us stop and think about what sort of picture we are presenting to each other."

THE QUEEN'S CHRISTMAS MESSAGE, 1962

If The Queen did not exactly 'swing' into the 1960s, she embraced its technology wholeheartedly and, to a somewhat lesser extent, its changing fashions – her hemline was raised above the knee.

PRINCE ANDREW

The Queen's third child, Prince Andrew Albert Christian Edward was born at Buckingham Palace on 19 February 1960 and christened in the palace's Music Room by the Archbishop of Canterbury, Geoffrey Fisher, on 8 April that year. Being the second son, he leap-frogged over his sister, Anne, to become second in line to the throne. (Subsequent births now place him fourth in the line of succession.) He was educated at Heatherdown in Ascot and Gordonstoun before he followed in his father's footsteps and enrolled at the naval college in Dartmouth, becoming a highly regarded helicopter pilot who saw active service in the Falklands.

IN THE 1960s

(Prices have been converted into decimal currency)

Prime ministers	Harold Macmillan (1957–63);
	Sir Alec Douglas-Home (1963–4);
	Harold Wilson (1964–70)
Price of a pint of milk	3.3p
Price of a loaf of bread	4.8p
Price of a dozen eggs	29.5p
Price of petrol	25p per gallon; 5.8p per litre
Average weekly wage	£24
Average house price	£3,600
On TV	Coronation Street;
	The Avengers; Z Cars;
	Steptoe and Son;
	Ready Steady Go!; Doctor Who;
	The Forsyte Saga;
	Civilisation; Take Your Pick;
	Double Your Money;
	The Black and White
	Minstrel Show

PRINCESS MARGARET'S WEDDING

Throughout her life The Queen's headstrong younger sister seemed to be a cause of anxiety and delight to her sovereign in equal measure. Artistic, musical, enormously sociable and devastatingly good-looking, the young Princess Margaret fascinated the press and kept the nation on tenterhooks as far as romance was concerned. Her first public romance was with a former equerry to King George VI, Group Captain Peter Townsend, a man who was regarded by the church and the establishment as 'unsuitable', due to the fact that he was divorced. In 1955, two years after the couple had first shown signs of their affections, she officially announced her decision not to marry him. It was a decision welcomed by the church (and, perforce, the Crown). The Princess was clearly in love with Townsend, but – unlike her Uncle David before her – put her country and her faith before herself:

> *... mindful of the Church's teaching that Christian marriage is indissoluble, and conscious of my duty to the Commonwealth, I have resolved to put these consider-ations before any others.*

The Archbishop of Canterbury, Geoffrey Fisher, rejoiced at her decision and consoled her by saying: "What a wonderful person the Holy Spirit is." She must have felt considerably reassured!

The following year Margaret met the society photographer Anthony Armstrong-Jones, and the Archbishop married them at Westminster Abbey on 6 May 1960 in front of 2,000 guests. Described as a 'fairytale wedding' (a term that would now ring alarm bells in the most optimistic of souls), the ceremony was televised and watched by 20 million people in the UK and an estimated audience of 300 million around the world. Princess Margaret, like her sister before her, was dressed by Sir Norman Hartnell and the wedding took place in glorious sunshine, after which the couple left for a honeymoon in the Caribbean on board HMY *Britannia*.

On the face of it the couple were well suited – both were arty, and he a touch Bohemian, which appealed to a Princess who often felt stifled by court etiquette (though ironically in later life she was a stickler for it more than most).

The groom's mother was formerly Anne Messel, sister of the designer Oliver Messel, and his father, Ronald Armstrong-Jones, was a barrister. Armstrong-Jones's parents divorced in 1934 and a year later his mother married the sixth Earl of Rosse. Though strictly speaking a commoner, Armstrong-Jones had noble if not regal connections. In 1961, The Princess's husband was created first Earl of Snowdon.

Though labelled a 'society photographer', and thought by some to be an unworthy match, Snowdon went on to establish himself as a hugely talented photographer, specializing in portraits, and also as a designer. His apotheosis would be the investiture of The Prince of Wales at Caernarfon Castle in 1969. Before and after that he was to immortalize many of the great with his camera, along with a number of royal weddings.

On their return to the UK the couple began their married life in apartments within Kensington Palace – the home of many lesser members of the royal family and consequently referred to as 'The Aunt Heap'. They provided interest for the gossip columns ever after.

THE QUEEN AND FASHION

At 5 ft 4 in The Queen is officially classed as 'petite', and while she is not totally immune to the whims of fashion her clothes must be suited to the job in hand. Off duty, at Sandringham or Balmoral, she is most frequently to be seen in a headscarf, tweed or tartan skirt, waterproof jacket or coat and stout lace-up shoes. She famously refuses to wear a hard hat when out riding – a pastime she still enjoys almost daily, except in cold winter weather as it now makes her eyes water.

For official occasions The Queen has always favoured bright or pastel colours so that she can be easily spotted in a crowd. The brims of hats must not conceal her face from view. Any umbrella that is carried when it is raining is likely to be transparent for the same reason. The Queen's job is to be seen.

Good tailoring, a brooch, a string of pearls and, most frequently, large single-pearl earrings topped with a single diamond (The Queen has pierced ears) are de rigueur, as is the famous handbag (usually made by Launer). Speculation abounds as to what it contains.

Her earliest couturier was Sir Norman Hartnell; later favourites included Sir Hardy Amies and, more recently, Stewart Parvin. The Queen's dresser, Liverpudlian Angela Kelly, has also been entrusted with designing both clothes and hats in the last few years. Except at investitures and on some other indoor occasions, The Queen always wears gloves.

State occasions and formal dinners demand full-length gowns, many of them encrusted with beads and semi-precious stones, and elbow-length gloves. And The Queen is not short of jewels – necklaces, tiaras, brooches, earrings and bracelets have been handed down from generation to generation. She is also likely to wear a garter sash and small portrait miniatures of older family members just below her left shoulder.

THE LINE OF SUCCESSION

Future legislation is likely to result in the firstborn of the monarch taking up a position as first in line to the throne, regardless of gender, but historically succession has followed the male line. As a result, this is the current line of succession:

1 The Prince of Wales
2 The Duke of Cambridge
3 Prince Henry of Wales
4 The Duke of York
5 Princess Beatrice of York
6 Princess Eugenie of York
7 The Earl of Wessex
8 Viscount Severn (son of The Earl of Wessex)
9 Lady Louise Mountbatten-Windsor (daughter of The Earl of Wessex)
10 The Princess Royal

PRINCE EDWARD

The Queen's last child, Prince Edward Anthony Richard Louis, was born at Buckingham Palace on 10 March 1964, and The Queen's pregnancy meant that she made her Christmas broadcast in 1963 on the radio. The young

Prince was baptized in the private chapel at Windsor Castle on 2 May 1964. At the age of seven he went to Gibbs School, then on to Heatherdown and, finally, like his father and brothers before him, to Gordonstoun where he became head boy in his last term. After a gap year abroad he read history at Jesus College, Cambridge and went on to work with Andrew Lloyd-Webber in the Really Useful Group, before founding his own film production company.

"I think we should remember that in spite of all
the scientific advances and great improvements in our
material welfare, the family remains as the focal point of
our existence. There is overwhelming evidence that those
who cannot experience full and happy family life
for some reason or another are deprived of a great
stabilizing influence in their lives."

THE QUEEN'S CHRISTMAS MESSAGE, 1965

A FAMILY IN THE SPOTLIGHT

There are those who maintain that the royal family is dysfunctional. Such analysis is for psychologists. It remains sufficient for this writer to suggest that they have had more than their fair share of ill luck when it comes to marriage breakdowns, but then there are few families in this day and age that can claim to have an unblemished record where marital harmony is concerned, and none has to suffer the same relentless degree of media intrusion and pressure. The Queen is also said to be 'cold and aloof'. That's a bit harsh. Alongside Queen Mary she seems positively jovial. But it must be remembered that she is Queen; her children bow or curtsey on meeting her. Of course this custom seems odd to anyone whose mother or father is not a king or queen. It is likely to have repercussions (a welcome degree of respect for one's elders for a start), but emotional restraint is not confined to monarchs and there are millions more families in Britain who are not as demonstrative as others. The Queen is not given to hugging and kissing everyone she meets, and in an age of double-kissing even slight acquaintances this can seem positively standoffish.

Each member of the family (apart from the most junior) has their own private office with a staff dedicated to organizing their public lives, but it is inevitable that the lines are blurred and that staff will also deal with familial issues. As well as being a family it is, as The Duke of Edinburgh put it, "The Firm".

What is certain is that The Queen regards her own immediate family as being of prime importance; she phoned her mother and her sister every day. When many of the family meet only once a year at official functions – Trooping the Colour or, more informally, at the Chelsea Flower Show – she is anxious that they should catch up. She is as judgemental of their actions as any other mother (and occasionally as disapproving) but every bit as loyal when it comes to sticking together.

While The Queen is given to controlling her emotions, she is most certainly not without humour, laughing at herself as well as being a famously good mimic – a gift inherited by The Prince of Wales. She finds it hard to understand the newspapers' fascination with the minutiae of royal life ("we are not Hollywood," she once remarked to me).

THE HOUSE OF WINDSOR

Until 1917 the royal family did not have a 'surname' as such. It was during the reign of King George V – when World War I broke out – that the family links with the German state of Saxe-Coburg and Gotha (which came from Prince Albert's father, The Duke of Saxe-Coburg and Gotha – Queen Victoria was, herself, from the House of Hanover) was regarded as sounding rather too Germanic for a nation that was at war with that country. King George V plumped for the altogether more British-sounding 'House of Windsor'

– reflecting the seat of all British monarchs since William the Conqueror. In 1960 The Queen let it be known that the descendants of her own immediate family would be known as 'Mountbatten-Windsor' in deference to The Duke of Edinburgh's ancestry.

SIR WINSTON CHURCHILL

Having served his country as prime minister during two terms of office – from 1940–5 and 1951–5, Sir Winston Churchill died on 24 June 1965 and was accorded a state funeral. A statesman of incomparable stature, Churchill saw the country through the Second World War and was The Queen's first prime minister. He left his country with an ongoing debt of gratitude and a fund of stories that summed up his wit, his wisdom and his love of Queen and country.

The Queen Mother, writing to The Queen, remarked: "What a privilege to have lived in his day – a truly great man," and the sovereign, whom he had served so well, must have been especially saddened.

At Churchill's state funeral the usual rules of precedence were set aside: the Churchill family arrived after and left before the monarch. As Robert Hardman remarks in his book *Our Queen*, it was "a small gesture but one of immense significance at such a carefully choreographed event".

Sir Winston Churchill's impact on his country was huge, and was reflected in the respect shown by the royal family after his death.

THE PROFUMO AFFAIR

In 1962, at the height of the Cold War, John ('Jack') Profumo, the Minister of War, was at the centre of one of the greatest political security scandals of the twentieth century. Profumo, who was married to the actress Valerie Hobson, met Christine Keeler, a call girl, at Cliveden, the stately home of Lord Astor in Buckinghamshire, and subsequently had a brief affair with her. What later came to light, and increased the severity of the situation, was that Keeler had also had a liaison with a naval attaché at the Russian Embassy, Yevgeny Ivanov, thus placing the minister in an even more compromising situation. Rumours of the affair came to light in 1962, and in 1963 Profumo denied in Parliament that he had had any kind of inappropriate relationship with Keeler. He later admitted to the liaison and in June 1963 – having committed the unforgivable sin of lying to parliament – resigned, effectively bringing down the Macmillan government. The prime minister resigned shortly after on the grounds of ill health. Profumo never spoke about the affair, but spent the rest of his life involved in charity work, receiving a CBE for his contribution to Toynbee Hall in London where he had worked tirelessly with the homeless and down-and-outs for 40 years until his death in 2006 at the age of 91.

THE ABERFAN DISASTER

On 21 October 1966 a spoil heap in the mining village of Aberfan in South Wales collapsed, engulfing houses and a local school. It was the worst mining disaster in living memory – 116 children and 28 adults were killed. The National Coal Board and Lord Robens, head of the board was taken to task for its attitude to the disaster. A disaster fund raised £1.6 million in a matter of months (equivalent to more than £20 million today). The survivors continue to mourn the passing of almost an entire generation in one day.

THE RISE OF TECHNOLOGY

At the start of The Queen's reign, many homes did not have a fridge or even an indoor lavatory. Phones and TV sets were for the privileged few, and central heating was the exception rather than the rule in most houses. But Prime Minister Harold Wilson's "white heat of technology" was about to make its mark.

1960   Plans are announced for a London Tidal Barrier – to be ready in six years.

The Cold War is still going strong.

The Queen launches the first nuclear submarine, *Dreadnought*.

1961   The E-type Jaguar is launched at £2,196.

Russian Yuri Gagarin becomes the first man in space with one orbit of the Earth. Alan Shepherd achieves the same feat three weeks later for the Americans but does not complete an orbit.

The millionth Morris Minor rolls off the production line.

1962   John Glenn orbits the earth for the Americans.

The first hovercraft enters service taking passengers and mail across the River Dee.

1963   The first successful kidney transplant.

The American Express credit card is launched in the UK.

1965   Crimplene (polyester) comes on to the market. (And it seemed so go-ahead ...)

The millionth Mini is sold.

Post Office Tower opens – the tallest building in Britain at 620 ft.

A 70 mph speed limit is introduced on motorways.

1966 The first soft landing on the Moon by Russian
spacecraft Luna 9.

The brain drain – British scientists seek more money
and better opportunities in the United States.

Barclaycard, the first British credit card, is introduced.

1967 The Queen launches QE2 at Clydebank.

The first heart transplant takes place in Cape Town.

The world's first cash dispensing machine is installed
by Barclays in Enfield.

The last steam trains are taken out of service.

1968 The breathalyzer comes into use.

The first British heart transplant is performed.

The two-tier postal service – first- and second-class mail
– is introduced.

1969 The maiden flight of British Concorde from Filton in
Bristol (airborne for 21 minutes).

First man on the Moon: American Neil Armstrong.
"One small step for a man ..."

Vasectomy operations start.

THE RED BOXES

On top of her regular commitments, at 7 p.m. each weekday evening, The Queen is presented with a red despatch box containing state papers. There may be up to 60 A4 sheets, which she needs to read, sign where necessary – indicating the royal assent – and otherwise digest. They are invariably finished and ready for despatch the next day. The Queen receives these red-leather-covered boxes every day except Christmas Day and Easter Day. On Fridays she receives a larger box for the weekend. The contents will include papers from the Cabinet and Foreign and Commonwealth Offices, summaries of the day in parliament, cabinet minutes and reports on 'developing situations' from British embassies around the world. The Prince of Wales has his own boxes, which are dark green.

THE CORGIS

The Queen has an association with Welsh corgis that dates back to 1933 when her father bought Rosavel Golden Eagle (thereafter known to the family as 'Dookie'). The Queen was given her favourite corgi Susan on her 18th birthday and more have followed over the years. Like many of the breed, 'Dookie' was famously snappy, and today The

Queen and her footmen have to break up many a set-to between the corgis and the 'dorgis' – crosses between corgis and dachshunds (the original dachshund belonged to Princess Margaret).

At the time of writing The Queen has four corgis – Linnet, Willow, Holly and Monty – and three dorgis – Cider, Candy and Vulcan. The Queen chooses all the names herself and needs footmen who don't mind walking her dogs and attending to canine discipline. The Queen walks and feeds her dogs herself whenever possible and has been spotted on at least one occasion wearing an Elastoplast as a result of intervening in a dog fight. The corgis are frequently in attendance at private lunches given by The Queen and The Duke; indeed they are the most effective warning for guests that Her Majesty is about to arrive – the corgis inevitably appear first! When a guest apologized for inadvertently treading on one of her dogs The Queen smiled and replied: "It serves him right for being the same colour as the carpet."

"This year I should like especially to speak to women. In many countries custom has decreed that women should play a minor part in public affairs. It is difficult to realise that it was less than 50 years ago that women in Britain were first given the vote, but Parliament was first asked to grant this 100 years ago. Yet in spite of these disabilities, it has been women who have breathed gentleness and care into the harsh progress of mankind. The struggles against inhuman prejudice, against squalor, ignorance and disease, have always owed a great deal to the determination and tenacity of women.

"In the modern world the opportunities for women to give something of value to the human family are greater than ever, because, through their own efforts, they are now beginning to play their full part in public life."

THE QUEEN'S CHRISTMAS MESSAGE, 1966

THE PROGRESS OF WOMEN

1951   A mass observation study of working-class homes in the London area shows that women are working an average of 15 hours per day doing housework, childcare, cooking and cleaning . A quarter of that time is spent in the kitchen.

Most women do their shopping on Friday and spend between ten shillings (50p) and £2 on food.

One house in three had no bath and one in 20 no piped water.

1955   Blue denim jeans (originally developed as workwear for US cowboys) are the new craze for women.

1957   At the State Opening of Parliament on 30 November The Queen announces the creation of Life Peerages for both sexes. Previously only men could be peers.

1958   The first female peers take their seats in the House of Lords. The last debutantes are presented at court. The tradition of coming out – upper-crust 'gels' being presented to the king or queen at the age of around 17, curtsying to the sovereign and generally announcing to the world of suitable 'chaps' that one was available – was regarded now as both old-fashioned and undesirable.

1959   Working-class women often prepare themselves to go out on a Friday or Saturday night by wearing curlers in their hair during the afternoon, covering their heads with diaphanous scarves to keep such creations in place.

1961   The 'beehive' hairdo is all the rage. Hair was back-combed into a towering dome and heavily lacquered to keep it in place. (It was developed in the US in 1960 where it was also known as the B-52, named after the bulbous nose of the B-52 bomber.)

1963　Russia puts the first woman in space – Valentina Tereshkova.

The Beatles roar up the charts with 'She Loves You'.

1964　Mary Quant introduces short skirts in bold patterns. Vidal Sassoon cuts Mary's hair into his own version of 'the bob' and she becomes a fashion icon.

'Boutiques' spring up in Chelsea.

1965　The first female High Court Judge is appointed.

Jean Shrimpton ('The Shrimp') is the top model of the time.

Hemlines are still rising: the mini-dress is now little more than a pelmet.

The taxman moves in to tax children's clothes since many women are now wearing garments designed for juveniles.

1966　Swinging London: Carnaby Street has joined Chelsea as the focus of all things 'groovy' and fashionable.

The mini-skirt is everywhere (even The Queen's hemline rises). Trouser-suits become fashionable.

Twiggy (Lesley Hornby) is the rising star of the fashion world. A six-and-a-half-stone cockney waif, she is paid 10 guineas an hour for modelling.

The contraceptive pill, which first became available in 1961, is bringing about a social revolution, and there is much talk – in this pre-AIDS generation – of 'free love'.

1967   'Flower power' is all the rage with clothing patterned like herbaceous borders. Long-haired youths are wearing floral kaftans and sporting beads and dark granny glasses.

'Make love, not war!' is the slogan of the swinging 1960s.

1969   'Dolly birds' (attractive, though usually heavily made-up young women) appear and the hemline lowers with the advent of 'the maxi-skirt'.

AND FOR THE GENTLEMEN...

1966   England beat West Germany 4–2 in the World Cup at Wembley Stadium. The Queen presents the trophy to team captain Bobby Moore of West Ham.

INVESTITURE OF THE PRINCE OF WALES

Prince Charles was nine years old when The Queen had conferred upon him the title of Prince of Wales – a style traditionally granted to the eldest son of a reigning monarch since the reign of King Edward III in 1337. She let it be known that the investiture would take place when he was old enough to understand its significance. On 1 July 1969, four months before his 21st birthday, that was deemed to be the case. Caernarfon Castle, begun in 1283 by King Edward I on his conquest of Wales, was chosen as a fitting place for the investing of the monarch's son with the insignia of the principality and the Earldom of Chester. His accoutrements were a sword, a newly fashioned coronet of Welsh gold, a mantle, gold ring and gold rod. The Prince's formal response to The Queen was made with the words:

> *I, Charles, Prince of Wales, do become your liege man of life and limb and earthly worship and faith and truth I will bear unto you to live and die against all manner of folks.*

Lord Snowdon was appointed Constable of the Castle at the time of the investiture and as such was responsible for much of the 'invented' pomp and ceremony surrounding it – the previous investiture of Prince Edward in 1911 at the same location having been beyond most people's living memory.

Snowdon was in charge, among other things, of the design of the scarlet chairs on which the 4,000 guests were seated, the transparent canopy under which the investiture took place, and his own costume as constable – a creation in Lincoln green which he later described as being a cross between "a cinema usherette from the 1950s and the panto character Buttons".

Not all of Snowdon's innovations were appreciated by traditionalists such as Sir Anthony Wagner, Garter King of

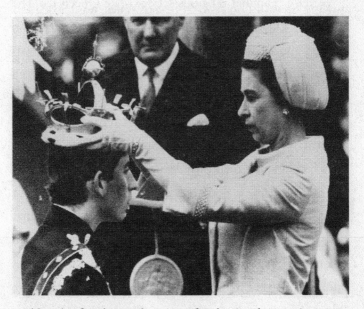

Although referred to as The Prince of Wales since he was nine years old, Charles waited a further twelve years for his investiture.

Arms, a man responsible for the College of Arms and as such the custodian of much of Britain's ceremonial heritage. Irked by Wagner's repeated inflexibility and intransigence Snowdon was overheard to remark at one moment of frustration: "Oh, come on Garter! Be a bit more elastic!"

A loyal address from the people of Wales was read in Welsh and English by the president of the University of Wales, Aberystwyth (where The Prince had spent a whole term studying the language and culture of the principality) and The Prince himself responded in both Welsh and English.

After a bilingual religious service, The Queen led The Prince to Queen Eleanor's Gate overlooking Caernarfon Castle's square and formally presented him to the crowds below, as members of his family looked on. The event itself passed off peacefully, but the day itself was not without drama – there were several attempted terrorist incidents, and two Welsh nationalists planting a bomb at Abergele were blown up by their own device.

The investiture occurred at what must have been a tricky time for The Prince – and indeed for any man: that no-man's land between adolescence and adulthood when the future (even for a man who would be King) seems uncertain and intimidating. At the time of the investiture Prince Charles was a student at Cambridge University. After studying archaeology and anthropology for a year

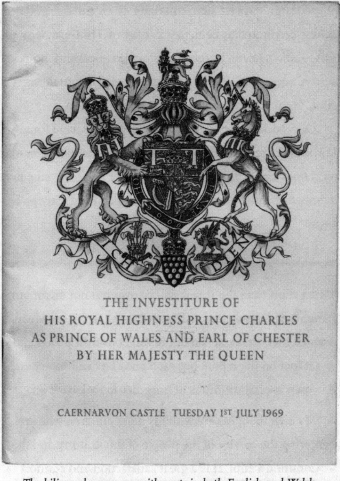

The bilingual ceremony, with parts in both English and Welsh, took place four months before Charles's 21st birthday.

he switched to history so that he could study the British Constitution. His endeavours in amateur dramatics while at university captured the attention of the media (one photograph showed him emerging from a dustbin), and he was celebrated as being a great fan of *The Goon Show* on BBC radio. There were serious achievements to be celebrated, too – that year he also made his first solo flight as a pilot. He was very much a young man of action.

One year on he would take his seat in the House of Lords and later that decade be invited by the prime minister, James Callaghan, to attend a cabinet meeting – the first member of the royal family to do so since King George I.

"In a short time the 1960s will be over but not out of our memories. Historians will record them as the decade in which men first reached out beyond our own planet and set foot on the moon, but each one of us will have our own special triumphs or tragedies to look back on.

"My own thoughts are with my older children who are entering the service of the people of this country and the Commonwealth. It is a great satisfaction and comfort to me and my husband to know they have won a place in your affections."

THE QUEEN'S CHRISTMAS MESSAGE (WRITTEN), 1969

THE ROYAL FAMILY FILM

The arrival of Prince Andrew and Prince Edward only added to the pressure on The Queen and The Duke to reveal more about their family in an age when television cameras were seemingly ubiquitous. Few organizations and institutions could resist their intrusion, and from 1958, when The Queen made it clear in her Christmas broadcast that she hoped to keep her children out of the spotlight's glare for as long as possible, the mood had been changing. Prince Philip particularly was in favour of a more open approach, and it was he who encouraged The Queen to agree to the making of the ground-breaking film *Royal Family* that showed the Windsors at work and play.

Unwanted press intrusion had begun much earlier. Prince Charles, then in his second year at Gordonstoun, had been followed by photographers while on a trip ashore at Stornoway on the Isle of Lewis where he ordered a cherry brandy in a local pub.

Long lenses began to appear whenever the royals were off duty. The Lord Chamberlain was relieved of his duty of censoring plays – leading to nudity and greater freedom of speech on stage in such plays as *Oh, Calcutta* and *Hair*. Princess Anne went to see the show in 1967 and her attendance was duly reported.

Prince Charles was not a natural broadcaster at the time when requests began pouring in for him to appear in front of the cameras in 1969 – the year of his proposed investiture as Prince of Wales at Caernarfon. It was decided that a film of all the family would be a good way to break the ice, and as a result, television cameras, under the guidance of producer Richard Cawston, followed the family in their daily life – both official and unofficial – from June 1968 to May 1969. The resulting film was broadcast by the BBC on 21 June 1969 and was watched by an audience of 23 million. It was repeated on ITV eight days later – two days before The Prince's investiture – by which time it was estimated that 68 per cent of the British public had seen it. The film was subsequently shown in 140 countries.

The sight of Prince Charles waterskiing and riding a bicycle, playing a cello and chatting with the family no doubt gave the watching public a better all-round view of the heir to the throne. They also enjoyed watching The Queen and her family decorate the family Christmas tree, feed the corgis, cook on a barbecue and generally behave as normally as they could in a royal palace and with the lens of a film camera upon them. The floodgates had been opened. Only time would tell whether or not sufficient light had been let in upon royalty 'to take away its magic'. One thing was proven beyond all doubt: having been given a glimpse into the royal world, from then on The Queen's subjects could never have enough of it – a state of affairs that even Walter Bagehot could not have foreseen.

TELEVISION IN THE 1960s

1961   *Children's Hour* was dropped from BBC radio schedules due to competition from television.

The enthronement of Dr Michael Ramsey as 100th Archbishop of Canterbury was broadcast on television.

1962   *The Avengers* made stars of Patrick Macnee and Honor Blackman.

1963   The Beatles released 'Please Please Me' and made their national TV debut on *Thank Your Lucky Stars*.

This year saw the start of the satirical TV show *That Was The Week That Was*, fronted by David Frost and attracting audiences of 12 million. It lampooned subjects that were previously taboo – sex, religion, politics and the monarchy – but was later taken off air in order to avoid its influencing the outcome of the following year's general election.

1964   Portable TV sets went on sale.

BBC2 began transmission.

Steptoe and Son topped the ratings, watched by 26 million viewers.

Ready Steady Go! cornered the youth market with weekly pop.

1965 Cigarette adverts are banned from TV.

   A poll showed that the English believed in God but preferred TV. (Churchgoing had fallen 14 per cent since 1957, while TV viewing figures had risen by 49 per cent.)

   Mary Whitehouse, having been campaigning to 'clean up TV' for 18 months, launched the National Viewers' and Listeners' Association and soon had half a million supporters in her quest to tackle 'bad taste'.

1967 Colour TV started.

1968 *The Forsyte Saga*, a dramatization of John Galsworthy's novels, became the most popular TV drama serial: church service times were adjusted to allow the congregation to get their weekly fix of Soames and Irene in the form of Eric Porter and Nyree Dawn Porter.

1969 *Civilisation*, Lord (Kenneth) Clark's 13-part series chronicling the artistic and cultural progress of western man began, resulting in him being referred to, tongue-in-cheek, as 'Lord Clark of Civilisation'.

THE COLD WAR

Though not actively involved in the so-called 'Cold War' – the frosty relationship between the east and west – The Queen was well aware of its possible consequences and kept fully informed of the state of relations between the respective superpowers at all times by her politicians and military chiefs of state. It was an unsettling time for the population; it must have been of particular concern to the nation's sovereign, whose knowledge of progress – or the lack of it – would have made her acutely aware of the 'real and present dangers'.

It was in the 1960s that the Cold War was at its height. The political conflict and military tension between the world's two biggest superpowers – the USSR (the communist Soviet Union and its satellite states) and the USA and its allies in the west – saw the start of the nuclear arms race and space race as the threat of nuclear war seemed ever more likely. This was the era of spies and espionage – the inspiration for countless thrillers. Though no direct head-to-head war was ever fought, the superpowers did support opposing sides in several proxy wars – Korea (1950–3), Vietnam (1959–75) and the Soviet war in Afghanistan (1979–89). In 1962 the American government, under President John F. Kennedy, attempted to oust communist President Fidel Castro's government on the uncomfortably close island of Cuba. The American invasion in the Bay of Pigs failed, and in retaliation Castro allowed the building of Soviet nuclear missile bases on his island – capable of striking targets in the USA. Only when the Russians agreed to dismantle and remove their nuclear weapons, and the Americans agreed never again to invade Cuba, did the situation cool down, but it led to the island being placed in quarantine – no Cuban goods (cigars included) came out and few foreign products (such as vehicle spare parts) went in. One of the outcomes was the creation of the telephone hotline between Moscow and Washington to allow the heads of state to talk directly to each other in the hope of avoiding future conflicts. The Cold War began in the late 1950s and ended – in theory – when the Soviet Union collapsed in 1991.

THE ARMS RACE

1952 Britain explodes its first nuclear bomb on an island north of Australia.

1958 The Campaign for Nuclear Disarmament (CND) is born and 600 people march from Aldermaston in Berkshire (where nuclear bombs were manufactured) to London in protest.

1960 The Queen launches Dreadnought, Britain's first nuclear-powered submarine.

A US spy plane piloted by Gary Powers is shot down over the USSR.

1961　The CND protest in Trafalgar Square – attended by, among others, George Melly, Vanessa Redgrave and John Osborne – results in violent clashes with 3,000 members of the police.

1962　The Cuban Missile Crisis brings the world to the brink of nuclear destruction – or so it seems.

Britain agrees to buy Polaris missiles.

1979　The Surveyor of The Queen's Pictures, Sir Anthony Blunt, is named 'the fourth man' (with Burgess, Maclean and Philby) involved in the Russian spy scandal that rocked the nation. He is stripped of his knighthood.

1983　The Greenham Common protestors – the 'Women for Life on Earth' – arrive and set up camp at the Berkshire airbase where 96 cruise missiles are to be sited. At one point 30,000 of them join hands to encircle the base and, despite repeated attempts to remove them, a determined few remain even after the missiles are removed in 1991.

2000　The 'Women's Peace' camp is finally disbanded after 19 years of continuous protest. The site at Greenham is now a business park.

"'Peace on Earth' – we may not have it at the moment; we may never have it completely, but we will certainly achieve nothing unless we go on trying to remove the causes of conflict between peoples and nations. 'Goodwill towards men' is not a hollow phrase. Goodwill exists, and when there is an opportunity to show it in practical form we know what wonderful things it can achieve.

"To deny this Christmas message is to admit defeat and give up hope. It is a rejection of everything that makes life worth living, and what is far worse it offers nothing in its place."

THE QUEEN'S CHRISTMAS MESSAGE, 1965

THE 1970s

"This year I am thinking of a rather special family –
a family of nations – as I recall fascinating
journeys to opposite ends of the world.

"During the course of these visits we met and talked with
a great number of people in every sort of occupation, and
living in every kind of community and climate. Yet in
all this diversity they had one thing in common: they
were all members of the Commonwealth family.

"Early this year we went to Fiji, Tonga, New Zealand and
Australia in *Britannia*. We were following the path taken
in 1770 by that great English discoverer, Captain Cook.
A little later in the year we were in Canada, still in the
Commonwealth, visiting the Northwest territories and
Manitoba for their centenaries. Among people who are
so essentially New Zealanders, Canadians or Australians,
it struck me again that so many of them still have
affectionate and personal links with the British Isles."

THE QUEEN'S CHRISTMAS MESSAGE, 1970

The Queen's genuine and practical dedication to the Commonwealth is in evidence time after time in her Christmas messages, and though much has happened in the 40-odd years since she spoke these words – with rumblings of disaffection in both Canada and Australia – those two countries maintain their Commonwealth links to this day. Much credit for this state of affairs belongs to The Queen herself (not that she would dream of taking the credit). As the Reagan, Gorbachev and Thatcher years proved, much can be achieved by disparate individuals if they have a common goal and – above all – mutual respect.

Within the European Union, at the time of writing, the common goal might be evident, but the mutual respect would seem to be thin on the ground. Perhaps the leaders of France, Germany, Greece and Italy could learn a little from an organization that was founded 60 years ago; a 'family' which shares common aims but which is also allowed to rejoice in its cultural differences.

IN THE 1970s

Prime ministers	Edward Heath (1970–4);
	Harold Wilson (1974–6);
	James Callaghan (1976–9)
Price of a pint of milk	4.7p
Price of a loaf of bread	8.8p
Price of a dozen eggs	23.2p
Price of petrol	73.2p per gallon; 16.3p per litre
Average weekly wage	£75
Average house price	£11,700
On TV	Emmerdale Farm;
	Nationwide;
	The Sweeney;
	Pebble Mill at One;
	The Morecambe and Wise Show;
	Fawlty Towers;
	Not the Nine O'Clock News;
	Rumpole of the Bailey;
	Monty Python's Flying Circus;
	To the Manor Born;
	Last of the Summer Wine

THE ROYAL TOURS

With an estimated 160,000 km (roughly 100,000 miles) in most years, The Queen is as well travelled as any international businessman. Not a year has gone by when she has not made at least one state visit – not pleasure trips but tightly structured and highly organized tours of cities, countries, work places and organizational headquarters, with luncheons, dinners and receptions an integral part of the day.

Tours take roughly two years to organize and every detail – from timings and distances to particular customs and protocol of the country being visited – are thoroughly examined. Each day runs to a tight timetable – The Queen can fulfil ten or more engagements in a typical day. The Duke may accompany her, or he may be diverted to other venues more suited to his interests, but the two will usually meet up at the end of the day at a dinner or reception that is attended by both. The day is likely to last 14 hours, during the course of which she will shake hundreds of hands and smile hundreds of smiles. (Should she ever be accused – as she sometimes is – of scowling or frowning, then she is probably just taking a break from the norm …)

Accompanied by her household – the entourage who make the arrangements and who accompany her on her travels – she will have gifts for her hosts (often examples of British craftsmanship) and a few home comforts – a feather pillow, bottled mineral water, a hot-water bottle, short-bread, plus tea and a kettle.

Foreign heads of state are more impressed by a visit from The Queen than from anyone else. She is, without doubt, the most famous person in the world, but she also comes from a family with a long and illustrious history – a royal family that has survived the tests of time while many others have been deposed or sent into exile. As one wag remarked: "In a few years there will be only five royal houses left in the world: hearts, clubs, diamonds, spades and Windsor."

The Queen often mentions her travels in Christmas broadcasts; one in particular stands out because of the touch of humour it contains. In 1958 The Queen's Christmas broadcast focused very much on journeys made by her and other members of the royal family round the Commonwealth. She mentions "In three weeks' time my husband goes to India and Pakistan and then on across the Pacific, my mother is going to East Africa, and my uncle, The Duke of Gloucester, and his wife will be travelling as my representatives to Nigeria. My aunt, The Duchess of Kent, and my cousin, Princess Alexandra, are also undertaking long journeys; together they will be visiting Central and South America in the spring and later Princess Alexandra goes to Australia to attend the centenary celebrations for the state of Queensland. In June my husband and I will be going to Canada once again. You'll remember that my sister Princess

Margaret was there earlier this year; this time we go primarily to open the great St Lawrence Seaway but we shall be visiting other parts of the country as well. Lastly, towards the end of the year we are going to Ghana and on the way back we intend to visit my people in Sierra Leone and the Gambia". A little later she adds: "We have no plans for space travel – at the moment."

ELIZABETH'S TOURS BEGAN BEFORE SHE BECAME QUEEN:

1947   Elizabeth accompanied her parents on a tour of South Africa and Rhodesia; she celebrated her 21st birthday in Cape Town.

1951   Elizabeth and Philip made a five-week coast to coast tour of Canada.

ROYAL TOURS SINCE BECOMING QUEEN:

1953/4   First Commonwealth tour; this was a pivotal tour for The Queen, and one which would be remarkable in that it was the longest overseas tour of her reign, lasting a total of almost seven months.

1955   State visit to Norway.

1956   State visits to Sweden and Nigeria.

1957   State visits to the USA, Portugal, France, Denmark.
        Visit to Canada in October during which The Queen
        opened the new Canadian parliament, the first time
        that any sovereign had done so.

1958   State visit to the Netherlands.

1959   State visit to the USA. Six-week Canadian tour, which
        included opening the St Lawrence Seaway.

1960   State visit to Denmark.

1961   State visits to Cyprus, India, Pakistan, Nepal, Iran,
        Ghana, Sierra Leone, the Gambia, Liberia and the
        Vatican.

1962   Visit to the Netherlands for the silver wedding
        anniversary of Queen Juliana and Prince Bernhard.

1963   Tour of New Zealand and Australia.

1964   Visit to Canada for the centenary celebrations.

1965   State visits to Ethiopia and Sudan and Germany.

1966   State visit to Belgium. Tour of the Caribbean.

1967   State visits to Canada and Malta.

1968   Visit to Chile and Brazil.

1969   State visit to Austria.

1970   Tour of Australia and New Zealand, visiting Fiji and
         Tonga en route.

1971   State visit to Turkey; visit to Canada.

1972   State visits to Thailand, Singapore, Malaysia, Brunei,
         the Seychelles and Maldives, Mauritius, Kenya,
         France and Germany.

1973   Visits to Australia and Canada.

1974   State visit to Indonesia; tour of New Zealand, South
         Sea Islands and Australia.

1975   State visits to Mexico and Japan via Hong Kong and
         Hawaii.

1976   State visits to Finland, Luxembourg and the USA.
         Visit to Canada to open the Olympic games.

1977   Tours of South Sea Islands, Australia, Canada and the
         West Indies.

1978   Visits to Germany and Canada.

1979   State visits to Saudi Arabia, Kuwait, Bahrain, Qatar, Oman, the United Arab Emirates, Denmark, and Africa.

1980   State visits to Switzerland, Italy, the Vatican, Morocco, Algeria, Tunisia, Belgium and Germany; visit to Australia.

1981   State visits to Norway, Sri Lanka. Visits to Australia and New Zealand.

1982   Visits to Canada, Australia and South Sea Islands.

1983   State visits to Sweden, Kenya, India and Bangladesh. Visits to Jamaica and the Cayman Islands, Mexico, the USA and Canada.

1984   State visit to Jordan. Visit to Canada and to France for the 40th anniversary of the D-day landings.

1985   Visit to the West Indies.

1986   State visit to Nepal and China. Visits to Hong Kong, Australia and New Zealand.

1987   Visits to Germany and Canada.

1988   State visit to Spain. Visits to the Netherlands and Australia.

1989 State visit to Singapore and Malaysia. Visit to Barbados.

1990 State visit to Iceland. Visits to New Zealand and Canada.

1991 State visits to the USA, Namibia and Zimbabwe.

1992 State visits to Germany, France, Malta. Visit to Australia.

1993 State visit to Hungary. Regimental visits to Cyprus and Germany.

1994 State visits to West Indies and Russia. Visit to Canada.

1995 State visit to South Africa. Visit to New Zealand.

1996 State visits to Thailand, Poland and the Czech Republic.

1997 State visit to India and Pakistan. Visit to Canada.

1998 State visits to Malaysia and Brunei. Visits to Belgium and France.

1999 State visit to Korea. Visits to South Africa, Ghana and Mozambique.

2000 State visit to Italy and the Vatican. Commonwealth visit to Australia.

2001 State visit to Norway.

2002 Commonwealth visits to Jamaica, Australia, New Zealand and Canada.

2003 Commonwealth visit to Nigeria.

2004 State visit to France.

2005 Commonwealth visits to Canada and Malta.

2006 State visit to Lithuania, Latvia and Estonia. Commonwealth visit to Australia and Singapore.

2007 State visits to the Netherlands, Belgium and the USA (to commemorate the 400th anniversary of the Jamestown settlement). Commonwealth visits to Malta and Uganda.

2008 State visits to Turkey, Slovenia and Slovakia.

2009 Commonwealth visits to Bermuda, Trinidad and Tobago.

2010 State visit to the USA (visiting Ground Zero). State visit to the United Arab Emirates and Oman. Commonwealth visit to Canada.

2011 State visit to Ireland. Commonwealth visit to Australia.

DECIMAL CURRENCY

Pounds, shillings and pence; ten bob, a guinea, half a crown, a tanner, a ha'penny, a farthing and a florin – all terms that disappeared from our lives when decimal currency came into being on 15 February 1971 – 'D-Day' as it was called (though the farthing had, to be strictly accurate, been withdrawn as legal tender in 1960 and the ha'penny (halfpenny) in 1969).

The public – especially those of the older generation – had some difficulty at first, and there was a cross-over period when prices would be indicated in both 'old' and 'new' money.

Old money	*Decimal equivalent*
Guinea (one pound and one shilling)	£1.05
One pound (240 old pence or 12 shillings)	£1.00
Ten shillings (ten bob)	50p
Five shillings (the old crown)	25p
Half a crown	12.5p
Florin (two shillings)	10p
Shilling (a bob)	5p

Sixpence (a tanner)	2.5p
Threepenny bit	1.25p
Penny (known as 'coppers' because of their colour and make-up)	(Replaced with 1p coins)
Ha'penny (halfpenny)	(Replaced with ½p coins)

Pound notes continued to be legal tender until 1988, while ten-shilling notes ceased to be so in 1971.

As ever, the new currency had The Queen's head on the front (obverse side) and a variety of emblems on the reverse. The emblems change from time to time, but the sovereign's head remains, immovable; it has been there since ancient times. What was good enough for a Roman emperor …

THE COMMON MARKET

There is a note of caution – perhaps wariness – in The Queen's Christmas Message of 1972, one which the intervening years have proved to be not without foundation. The Economic Community was set up at the end of World War II with the aim of ending the conflicts that had been so prevalent in Europe over the preceding centuries. There were various landmarks:

1950   The European Coal and Steel Community (ECSC)
       was formed between France, Germany, Belgium, Italy,
       Luxembourg and the Netherlands.

1957   The Treaty of Rome created the Common Market
       or European Economic Community (EEC). Britain
       decided not to join, mindful of its own links with
       the Commonwealth and fearful that such a gigantic
       authority would erode Britain's sovereignty over its
       domestic affairs.

1961   Doubts were set aside and Britain made a bid to join
       the Common Market.

1963   President de Gaulle of France says 'non' to British EEC
       membership. The Queen cancels Princess Margaret's
       state visit to France.

1967   De Gaulle says 'non' once more.

       The abolition of customs duties between member
       countries results in massive food surpluses – 'butter
       mountains' and 'wine lakes'.

1972   Britain finally signs up to the EEC. (President de Gaulle
       died in 1970.)

1973   Britain joins the EEC, along with Denmark and Ireland.

1975 The public vote 'yes' in the referendum on whether the UK should remain in the EEC.

1980 Mrs Thatcher gets tough and demands a cut in Britain's payments to the EEC budget.

1981 Greece becomes the 10th member of the EEC.

1989 The Berlin Wall comes down; the border between East and West Germany is open for the first time in 28 years.

1990 The reunification of Germany.

Environmental concerns shared by EEC members.

1993 The Maastricht Treaty came into force (in spite of most politicians not having read the massive document) and the word 'Economic' is dropped from the EEC to create the European Union (EU). The treaty aims to control inflation and stabilize exchange rates. The Single Market is completed bringing freedom of movement of money, goods, people and services across EU borders.

1995 Austria, Finland and Sweden join the EU.

The Schengen Agreement allows people to travel between EU countries without having their passports checked at borders.

1996   Spain and Portugal join the EU.

The BSE crisis – the European Commission bans the export of British beef.

2002   The Euro becomes the new currency in 12 of the 15 EU countries. Britain decides to keep the pound.

2004   Central and eastern European countries join the EU, along with Cyprus and Malta.

2011   Monetary crises in Greece, Italy, Portugal and Ireland severely test the alliance.

AS OF 2011 THE MEMBER STATES OF THE EU ARE:

Austria, Belgium, Bulgaria, Cyprus, Czech Republic, Denmark, Estonia, Finland, France, Germany, Greece, Hungary, Ireland, Italy, Latvia, Lithuania, Luxembourg, Malta, Netherlands, Poland, Portugal, Romania, Slovakia, Slovenia, Spain, Sweden, United Kingdom.

THOSE APPLYING AT THIS TIME:

Turkey, Croatia, former Yugoslav Republic of Macedonia, Montenegro and Iceland.

SILVER WEDDING

With the Silver Jubilee – 25 years since the accession of Queen Elizabeth II – only five years away, The Queen and The Duke's silver wedding anniversary in 1972 was a relatively low-key affair, but one which did not pass the public by. Typically, in her Christmas Message of that year, The Queen used it as an occasion not only to give thanks for her own family life, but also that of the Commonwealth:

> *My whole family has been deeply touched by the affection you have shown to us when we celebrated our silver wedding, and we are especially grateful to the many thousands who have written to us and sent us messages and presents. One of the great Christian ideals is a happy and lasting marriage between man and wife, but no marriage can hope to succeed without a deliberate effort to be tolerant and understanding. This doesn't come easily to individuals and it certainly doesn't come naturally to communities or nations. The new links with Europe will not replace those with the Commonwealth. They cannot alter our historical and personal attachments with kinsmen and friends overseas. Old friends will not be lost; Britain will take her Commonwealth links into Europe with her. Britain and these other European countries see in the Community a new opportunity*

for the future. They believe that the things they have
in common are more important than the things which
divide them, and that if they work together not only they,
but the whole world, will benefit.

A thanksgiving service was held in Westminster Abbey and a
25p coin (the equivalent of the old commemorative crown)
was produced to celebrate the event. It was one of only four
such coins produced – the others are:

1977 – Silver Jubilee
1980 – The Queen Mother's 80th birthday
1981 – Wedding of Prince Charles and Lady Diana
         Spencer

Commemorative coins after this date were given a face value
of £5, since the 25p value of the 'crowns'; was no longer
sufficient to cover the cost of their manufacture.

While endeavouring to support the broader aims of
the European Union, Britain's little battles go on – against
edicts from the headquarters of the EU in Brussels against
such things as bent cucumbers, selling bananas by the pound
instead of the kilo and the banning of old varieties of vege-
table seeds. For gardeners, there are continual frustrations;
but on a wider scale, worries over the national debt crises of
Greece, Italy, Ireland and Portugal pose an ongoing threat

to European stability. When asked in the autumn of 2011 what was going to happen in the long term, the Governor of the Bank of England confessed: "The long term? I don't even know what's going to happen tomorrow."

PRINCESS ANNE

Princess Anne's engagement was announced on 29 May 1973. Her choice of husband was an unusual one – not someone from the aristocracy (a foreign prince was no longer expected), but an upper-middle-class fellow equestrian – Lieutenant (later Captain) Mark Phillips of The Queen's Dragoon Guards. Both were exceptional in their horsemanship (soon after leaving school The Princess qualified for the Badminton Horse Trials and won the European Individual Championship in 1971). The marriage took place at Westminster Abbey on 14 November 1973 – Prince Charles's birthday.

It was a glittering affair – the groom in his Dragoon Officer's uniform and The Princess a vision in a white gown. Being the first child of the sovereign to marry, children were given a day off school to mark the occasion.

The couple went on to have two children, both born in St Mary's Hospital, Paddington: Peter Mark Andrew Phillips (15 November 1977) and Zara Anne Elizabeth

Phillips (15 May 1981). The Princess made it clear that neither of her children would take up a title, but would be known simply by their Christian names and surnames.

Peter Phillips worked for Jaguar, then Williams Formula One before taking up a post with the Royal Bank of Scotland. On 17 May 2008 he married the Canadian Autumn Kelly, at St George's Chapel, Windsor, and The Queen's first great-grandchild, Savannah, was born on 29 December 2010.

Zara's career as a horsewoman keeps her more in the public eye. She won the Eventing World Championships in 2006, and was awarded the MBE in 2007. Adding to her sporting achievements, on 30 July 2011 she married the England rugby captain Mike Tindall at Canongate Kirk in Edinburgh. Reports that the bride's mother suggested to the groom that he did something about his broken nose before the wedding are unconfirmed!

Princess Anne was created Princess Royal (see page 146) in 1987 and she is one of the busiest members of the royal family, with over 600 engagements a year and usually at least three major overseas tours. She is an active patron and supporter of over 200 organizations and 23 service units around the world.

Alas, in 1989 The Princess's marriage to Mark Phillips failed. The couple separated and were finally divorced in April 1992.

In 1992, The Princess Royal married Commander Tim Laurence (now Vice Admiral Sir Timothy Laurence), a naval officer and formerly an equerry to The Queen, at Crathie Kirk near Balmoral in Scotland.

Many find The Princess Royal a hard nut to crack. It's true that she can be exacting and, depending on her mood, somewhat abrupt. Like others in the public eye she can be intolerant of the press – especially when she views their actions as being intrusive. Hers was a conscious decision to keep her children out of the limelight – they are far enough down the line of succession to have lives of their own.

Despite these considerations, The Princess's sense of humour is well developed, dry and laconic and she is an extremely good speaker. Catch her on a good day and she is bright and stimulating company. On a bad day? Well, you'd best lie low. The great thing about her is that you will always know where you are.

She is now carrying out a number of the duties and patronages formerly undertaken by The Duke of Edinburgh – among them, several university chancellorships and the role of Master of Trinity House – the organization responsible for Britain's lighthouses and navigational aids. A keen sailor, she has been patron of the Northern Lighthouse Board (responsible for Scotland's lighthouses) since 1993, and is gradually ticking off visits to all her 'charges'. She now has a few hundred more to add to the list, but is unlikely to be daunted in her quest. She's not that sort of woman.

THE PRINCESS ROYAL

Princess Anne received the title 'Princess Royal' from The Queen in 1987. She is the seventh holder of the title, customarily but not automatically awarded to the sovereign's eldest daughter.

The title came into existence in the seventeenth century when Queen Henrietta-Maria (1609–1669), wife of King Charles I (1600–1649) and daughter of Henry IV of France, wanted to emulate the title given to the eldest daughters of the Kings of France: 'Madame Royale'.

PRINCESS ROYAL

The holders of the title:

Mary, eldest daughter of Charles I (1631–60)

Anne, eldest daughter of George II (1709–59)

Charlotte, eldest daughter of George III (1766–1829)

Victoria, eldest daughter of Queen Victoria (1840–1901)

Louise, eldest daughter of Edward VII (1867–1931)

Mary, eldest daughter of George V (1897–1965)

Anne, eldest daughter of Elizabeth II (1950–)

ALL THE QUEEN'S HORSES

The Queen was given her first pony – a Shetland called Peggy – when she was four years old. It was a gift from her grandfather, King George V. Her love of, and passion for, horses has continued ever since. Taught to ride by Owen, the groom at Windsor, she still rides out most mornings with her current groom Terry Pendry. When asked what they talk about Terry says: "Anything and everything."

Some of The Queen's happiest times have been spent riding in Windsor Great Park, where she prefers to ride in a headscarf rather than a hard hat. It would take a brave man …

At The Queen's first Trooping the Colour on 5 June 1953 she rode the police horse Winston, wearing the uniform of the Colonel-in-Chief of the Scots Guards. At leisure The Queen rides astride her horse, but for Trooping the Colour she rode sidesaddle – most usually on her favourite horse, Burmese (a gift from the Royal Canadian Mounted Police in 1969), until the mare was retired in 1986, after which The Queen took her place in the procession wearing civilian clothes and riding in a horse-drawn phaeton.

In 1981 The Queen displayed immense cool and courage, let alone superb horsemanship – when six shots were fired in her direction during the Trooping ceremony. Burmese was clearly unnerved by the incident, but The Queen quickly regained control. It turned out that the shots were blanks, fired by a youth protesting about unemployment.

Whether it is the horses in the Royal Mews, where such names as Lusaka and Alderney are given to the greys used to pull the coaches and carriages, or her mounted regiments – the Household Cavalry and the King's Troop Royal Horse Artillery (she asked that they retained their title after King George VI's death), The Queen's interest in them remains intense and active.

THE ROYAL WINDSOR HORSE SHOW

Held each May in the grounds of Windsor Castle for the last 65 years, this event is often attended by The Queen on each of the five days of its duration. It is the largest outdoor equestrian show in Britain with over 3,000 horses and ponies taking part in 250 classes. Dressed informally in a coat and headscarf and usually with the Crown Equerry, Colonel Toby Browne, and Master of the Horse, Lord Vestey, in tow, The Queen wanders among the crowd and watches the various competitions – show jumping, dressage and carriage driving – with a keen eye. The Duke of Edinburgh, though no longer taking part in competitive carriage driving, will still take the reins and rides out most mornings either at Windsor or Sandringham, and he acts as a timekeeper at the Windsor Show on the water splash. "A difficult task?" I ask innocently. "It's not rocket science," he exclaims, holding up his stopwatch. "You just press the button." (Ask a silly question …) But he clearly enjoys it, and the rapport between The Duke and the other judges is easy and relaxed.

On the last few evenings of the horse show the Windsor Castle Royal Tattoo is held – an extravaganza in the Castle Arena featuring horses, riders and servicemen from all over the world. The Queen and The Duke attend on the last evening – it's a moving spectacle and one enjoyed by the crowd and the royals alike.

THE TURF

Racing is another big royal interest. For The Queen Mother it was steeplechasing, but for The Queen flat racing is her bag. Whether it be the Derby at Epsom or Royal Ascot, The Queen is there – often watching her own horses, whose jockeys wear her own colours – a purple body with gold frogging and scarlet sleeves, along with a black cap fringed with gold.

The Queen inherited 20 mares from her father (The King was not especially interested in racing, but anxious that the staff of his stables should not be made redundant). The Queen's horse Aureole (bred by her father) finished second in the Derby at Epsom the day after her wedding. A win in the Derby has so far eluded her, but her knowledge of bloodlines and her interest in breeding may well yet see her succeed. What she does not know about horses and their breeding is, according to those who work for her, not worth knowing. Prince William tells me that, as a child, nervous about conversational topics with his grandmother, talking to her about horses would be guaranteed to make her eyes light up. When Winston Churchill was asked what he and The Queen talked about at their weekly Tuesday evening meetings he replied, "Racing mostly."

Lord Porchester (later Lord Carnarvon) was from 1967 The Queen's racing manager. Known as 'Porchie' he was a close friend of The Queen and much mourned at his death in 2001 at the age of 77.

Visits to Kentucky, Virginia and Wyoming have all been hugely enjoyed, and the Royal Studs at Sandringham and Polhampton, near Newbury, continue with The Queen's breeding programme – the horses then being sent out to trainers such as Sir Henry Cecil at Newmarket. Currently The Queen has around 25 horses in training each year, under royal racing manager John Warren.

ROYAL ASCOT

The Queen attends the Royal Ascot meeting each June riding down the course in a procession of open carriages from Windsor Castle where she hosts a house party for the week. The meeting dates back to 1711 and was founded by Queen Anne. Famous for its fashion as much as its horses, it continues to be a highlight of The Queen's calendar (though The Duke might well be found at the back of the royal box watching the cricket on television).

Prize money of around £4 million is awarded over the week, the major race being the Ascot Gold Cup, which is run on Ladies' Day – the Thursday.

Though The Queen Mother was a steeplechase fan, flat racing has always been more to The Queen's interest.

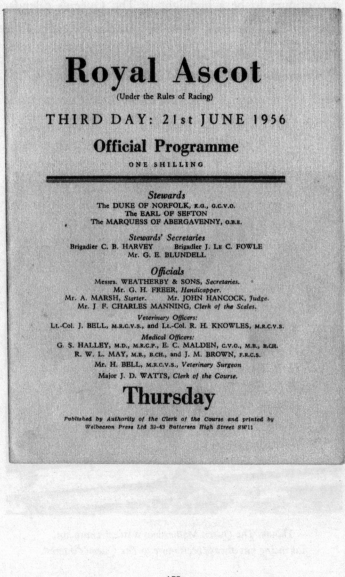

Royal Ascot

(Under the Rules of Racing)

THIRD DAY: 21st JUNE 1956

Official Programme

ONE SHILLING

Stewards
The DUKE OF NORFOLK, K.G., G.C.V.O.
The EARL OF SEFTON
The MARQUESS OF ABERGAVENNY, O.B.E.

Stewards' Secretaries
Brigadier C. B. HARVEY   Brigadier J. LE C. FOWLE
Mr. G. E. BLUNDELL

Officials
Messrs. WEATHERBY & SONS, *Secretaries.*
Mr. G. H. FREER, *Handicapper.*
Mr. A. MARSH, *Starter.*   Mr. JOHN HANCOCK, *Judge.*
Mr. J. F. CHARLES MANNING, *Clerk of the Scales.*

Veterinary Officers:
Lt.-Col. J. BELL, M.R.C.V.S., and Lt.-Col. R. H. KNOWLES, M.R.C.V.S.

Medical Officers:
G. S. HALLEY, M.D., M.R.C.P., E. C. MALDEN, C.V.O., M.B., B.CH.
R. W. L. MAY, M.B., B.CH., and J. M. BROWN, F.R.C.S.

Mr. H. BELL, M.R.C.V.S., *Veterinary Surgeon*

Major J. D. WATTS, *Clerk of the Course.*

Thursday

*Published by Authority of the Clerk of the Course and printed by
Welbecson Press Ltd 39-43 Battersea High Street SW11*

HOUSEHOLD BRIGADE POLO CLUB

Ascot Week Tournament

Polo will be played every evening on Smith's Lawn, Windsor Great Park, commencing at 5.30 p.m.

Entrance will be by Blacknest Gate, Bishopsgate Gate, and Cranbourne Gate only. The routes to these gates will be signposted.

Daily vouchers for the Members Enclosure will be sold in the Royal Ascot Enclosure and Car Passes are also on sale from a special Box in the Paddock situated between the Parade Ring and the Totalisator Building.

Dating back to 1711, when it was founded by Queen Anne, Royal Ascot is an annual institution, and Europe's most popular race meeting.

The Ascot dress code prevails in the Royal Enclosure – women must wear hats or not insubstantial fascinators, with no bare shoulders or midriff, and dresses must be of a suitable length – no mini-skirts. Gentlemen are expected to wear morning dress with waistcoat and top hat. With over 300,000 attending during the week, Royal Ascot is Europe's most popular race meeting.

THE DERBY

More correctly know as the Derby Stakes, the Epsom Derby is a flat race open to three-year-old colts and fillies, run over a distance of 1 mile, 4 furlongs, 10 yards. It is run each year on the first Saturday in June on the famous racecourse on Epsom Downs. Established in 1780 it is the richest race in Britain with a prize fund of around £1.25 million. It is one of Britain's five classic horse races and along with the 2,000 Guineas Stakes at Newmarket and the St Leger at Doncaster makes up what is known as the Triple Crown. (The other two classics are the 1,000 Guineas Stakes at Newmarket and the Epsom Oaks.) The Queen has so far failed to win the Derby – her horse Carlton House was the favourite in the 2011 race but finished third. Perhaps in her Diamond Jubilee year fate might smile upon her.

PRINCESS MARGARET'S DIVORCE

In 1978 The Queen's sister became the first member of the royal family to divorce since King Henry VIII. She and Lord Snowdon had separated in 1976 and Snowdon went on to marry Lucy Lindsay Hogg, a marriage which ended in divorce in 2000. The lives of both Lord Snowdon and Princess Margaret continued to fascinate the gossip columns, both enjoying lives that qualified in every way for the word 'colourful'.

During the 16 years of their marriage the royal couple had two children, David, Viscount Linley (b. 1961; m. Hon. Serena Stanhope, 1993) and Sarah (b. 1964; m. Daniel Chatto, 1994).

The Princess never remarried, though her romantic attachments continued to be the subject of speculation until her death on 19 February 2002.

"We are an inventive and tenacious people and the comradeship of adversity brings out the best in us."

THE QUEEN'S CHRISTMAS MESSAGE, 1974

HARD TIMES, UNEMPLOYMENT AND INFLATION

The 1960s had seen the rise of youth culture and prosperity – rationing was no more and living standards were rising rapidly. Ordinary families started taking holidays abroad, they had fridges, central heating, and maybe even a car and a telephone. But the 1970s were, in general, a time of industrial unrest, strikes and recession. Industrial output was down and Britain's place in the world not as powerful as it had once been. In one year alone, strikes wiped out 10 million working days. Even gravediggers went on strike. And there was worse to come …

HARD TIMES

1970   Edward Heath wins the election for the Conservatives.

1971   Rolls Royce is declared bankrupt; Upper Clyde Shipbuilders is forced into liquidation.

Postal workers go on strike for the first time in history, asking for a 19.5 per cent pay rise.

Fax machines become hugely popular.

Margaret Hilda Thatcher, Education Secretary, plans to end free school milk, giving rise to the slogan: 'Margaret Thatcher, milk snatcher'.

1972   The Miners' Strike leads to power cuts nationwide with blackouts lasting up to nine hours at a time. Coal-fired power stations run out of fuel.

1973   Foreign cars now outsell those of British Leyland.

The government declares a state of emergency as strikes by power workers, miners and railwaymen continue. The Arab-Israeli War makes things even worse when oil supplies are affected. TV goes off the air at 10.30 p.m. to reduce electricity consumption, and a 50 m.p.h. speed limit is imposed on motorways to restrict the use of petrol. Petrol ration books are issued but ultimately not brought into use.

1974   Industry is working a three-day week; half a million workers are laid off.

Edward Heath is defeated in the election and Harold Wilson returns, vowing to get Britain "back to work". Runaway inflation follows – petrol increases from 42p to 72p per gallon.

1975   Britain's second largest oil company – Burmah – collapses.

Inflation hits 25 per cent.

The miners end their strike after being offered a 35 per cent pay rise.

Wilson's 'social contract' with the unions fails.

Pay rises to be limited to £6 a week.

Margaret Thatcher becomes the new Tory leader, defeating Edward Heath.

1976 A slide in the value of sterling forces the government to take out a £2.3 billion loan from the IMF.

James Callaghan becomes Prime Minister.

1977 British Leyland is hit by strikes: for the first time, Britain imports more cars than it makes. We import far more goods than we manufacture at home.

Unemployment reaches 2 million (a figure not matched since the 1930s).

1978 The government announces a 15 per cent cap on pay increases, which the unions reject as unrealistic.

Car workers at Ford put in for a £20-a-week pay increase, which the government rejects. By September all their car plants are on strike.

The Winter of Discontent – widespread strikes, rubbish piling up in the streets, shortages of food and petrol. James Callaghan declares that it is "make or break" for his government.

Unemployment stands at over 2 million.

1979   Margaret Thatcher wins the election (and stays in
        No.10 until 1990).

NOT THAT IT WAS ALL BAD NEWS ...

1970   The first Jumbo jet lands at Heathrow.

        North Sea oil is discovered by BP.

        The first heart pacemaker goes into use.

        Women's Lib gains momentum.

        The Prince of Wales graduates and makes his first
        speech at the Cambridge Union, raising concerns about
        the environment and pollution.

        The New English Bible is published.

1971   Astronauts drive on the Moon.

        Hot pants (short shorts) are the last word in women's
        fashion.

1973   The wedding of Princess Anne to Captain Mark
        Phillips creates a rush for colour TV sets, but they
        are so expensive and unreliable that most folk opt for
        renting them.

        Prince Charles is formally installed as Duke of Cornwall
        at Launceston Castle.

1975   North Sea oil starts flowing.

       International Women's Year: the Sex Discrimination
       Act comes into being.

1977   Sir Freddie Laker's cut-price Skytrain comes into
       service: a flight from London to New York costs £59
       (meals extra).

1978   The first test-tube baby is born in a Greater Manchester
       hospital.

       North Sea oil output reaches 1 million barrels a day.

1979   British scientist Sir Godfrey Hounsfield wins the
       Nobel Prize in Physiology for the invention of the
       CT body scanner.

"I shall never forget the scene outside Buckingham
Palace on Jubilee Day. The cheerful crowd was symbolic
of the hundreds and thousands of people who greeted us
wherever we went this Jubilee year – in 12 Commonwealth
countries and 36 counties in the United Kingdom."

THE QUEEN'S CHRISTMAS MESSAGE, 1977

THE SILVER JUBILEE

Despite occurring during a time of recession, 1977 saw Britain awash with bunting to celebrate The Queen's 25 years on the throne. The Jubilee celebrations gave many of us the chance to forget, temporarily, the misery of unemployment and the difficulties of being strapped for cash. The Queen declared that unity was to be the theme of her Silver Jubilee and she aimed to be as visible to as many of her UK subjects as possible. Her tour of Britain began in Scotland and ended ten weeks later in Northern Ireland. On the evening of 6 June The Queen lit a huge bonfire in Windsor Great

Despite taking place during a recession,
the Silver Jubilee saw nationwide celebrations.

Park, which was followed by a chain of 100 other beacons across the country, many of them on the same spots as those that were lit to celebrate the defeat of the Spanish Armada during the reign of Elizabeth I in 1588.

On Tuesday 7 June The Queen and Prince Philip took the Golden State Coach to a service of thanksgiving at St Paul's Cathedral. Millions lined the route and 500 million around the world watched on television. An appearance on the balcony of Buckingham Palace followed and street parties – an estimated 4,000 of them in London alone – filled the rest of the day. Commemorative stamps were issued and a river procession took place along the Thames from Greenwich to Lambeth, culminating in the opening of the Silver Jubilee walkway by The Queen and a return to Buckingham Palace in lighted carriages.

The punk rock band the Sex Pistols attempted to get in on the act by sailing down the river and playing their irreverent version of 'God Save The Queen'. They were arrested on disembarking. Still, the record did get to No. 2 in the charts, in spite of being banned by the BBC. The original version, however, has lasted rather longer.

As if to crown the occasion, on The Queen's visit to the lawn tennis championships at Wimbledon (a rare occurrence) the ladies' singles championship was won by Virginia Wade who beat Betty Stove of the Netherlands 4-6, 6-3, 6-1 to become the first British champion since Ann Jones

*A host of celebratory souvenirs were created,
and badges were worn with pride.*

in 1969. Knowing that The Queen was due to attend the finals, Wade told herself: "If she's going to be there, I'm going to be there, and if I'm going to be there I might as well win." Nine years later she was awarded the OBE.

"If you throw a stone into a pool, the ripples go on spreading outwards. A big stone can cause waves, but even the smallest pebble changes the whole pattern of the water. Our daily actions are like those ripples; each one makes a difference, even the smallest.

"It does matter, therefore, what each individual does each day. Kindness, sympathy, resolution and courteous behaviour are infectious. Acts of courage and self-sacrifice, like those of the people who refuse to be terrorized by kidnappers or hijackers, or who diffuse bombs, are an inspiration to others.

"And the combined effect can be enormous. If enough grains of sand are dropped into one side of a pair of scales they will, in the end, tip it against a lump of lead. We may feel powerless alone but the joint efforts of individuals can defeat the evils of our time."

THE QUEEN'S CHRISTMAS MESSAGE, 1975

NORTHERN IRELAND

'The troubles', as they are always called, refer to 300 years of religious conflict and Ireland's uneasy relationship with the British Crown. At the beginning of the twentieth century, Ireland – still undivided – was experiencing a revival of its national identity and there were growing demands for home rule, while remaining a part of the British Empire. The British government proposed home rule for Ireland – a move backed by the Catholic population but opposed by the Protestants. Only in Ulster was the Protestant population large enough to oppose the idea effectively.

In the Easter Rising of 1916 the Irish Republican Brotherhood led an insurrection against British rule, attacking the seat of power at Dublin Castle and declaring an Irish Republic. British troops intervened, rebel leaders were captured and 14 of them executed. The subsequent imposition of martial law led to the radicalization of many men who became volunteers in the Irish Republican Army.

In the election of 1918, Sinn Fein (the Irish National Party formed in 1905) triumphed and set up a republic under Eamon de Valera. The conflicts that followed led to many deaths, and in 1920 King George V signed an act of Parliament partitioning Ireland and creating two parliaments – one for 26 counties in southern Ireland, and the other for the six counties of Ulster in Belfast.

Still the unrest continued, with Sinn Fein failing to recognize the South's parliament when the Irish Free State was formed making Southern Ireland a dominion and, as such, a part of the Commonwealth.

In 1923 the civil war ended, but in Ulster retribution against the Catholics continued, with many of them driven out.

By the 1930s the country was stagnating and grew poorer, causing half a million people to leave and make new homes either on the British mainland or in the United States.

During the present Queen's reign the hostilities were especially prevalent during the 1960s and 1970s with riots in Londonderry, bombing campaigns in mainland cities and the murder of The Queen's cousin, Lord Louis Mountbatten, near his home at Classiebawn Castle in Ireland in August 1979. In October 1984 the IRA planted a bomb in the Grand Hotel in Brighton, which killed five people and injured 30 more.

Peace initiatives were made with the Anglo-Irish Agreement of 1985 under Margaret Thatcher and the Downing Street Declaration of 1993 under John Major, but the latter faltered in 1995 with differences of opinion over whether Sinn Fein should be included in all-party talks before the IRA and other paramilitary groups had begun to decommission their weapons.

In 1997 Sinn Fein President Gerry Adams and its deputy leader Martin McGuinness were elected to seats in Westminster but refused to swear allegiance to the British Crown and so did not take up their seats.

On 10 April 1998 – Good Friday – Republicans and Unionists agreed to a deal that would give the people of Northern Ireland the right to decide their own future democratically and end 30 years of bloodshed. 'The Good Friday Agreement', it was hoped, would bring lasting peace to the province. There were still occasional challenges to this process, but on 26 September 2005 the IRA finally disarmed. After 30 years and over three and a half thousand deaths there is peace in Ireland today and the visit of The Queen in May 2011 – the first by a British monarch in 100 years – was regarded by the entire country as a step forward. She could not have been better received, or her actions been more highly thought of.

FAMILY LOSSES

The 1970s saw the loss of two members of The Queen's immediate family – The Duke of Windsor in 1972 and Lord Louis Mountbatten in 1979. Both were tragic in their own way. The Duke's death, at the age of 77, brought an end to his exile in France, where he had lived since the end of the war with the woman for whom he renounced the throne. The Duchess of Windsor survived her husband by 14 years – living out her long and lonely life presided over by the fiercely protective chatelaine, Madame Blum. When The Duchess died on 24 April 1986 her body was brought to Britain and buried alongside that of her husband, at Frogmore in the grounds of Windsor Castle.

The Queen had visited The Duke – while on a state visit to France – just nine days before his death. Already very ill, and being nursed at the Windsors' home in the Bois de Boulogne, The Duke insisted that he would not receive his sovereign while lying in bed – despite being on an intravenous drip. The Duke met The Queen fully dressed and sitting in a chair in the sitting room alongside his bedroom. To the consternation of his doctor, as The Queen entered the room The Duke stood up, almost dislodging the drip, whose apparatus was concealed behind a curtain. It was a brief meeting, lasting just a quarter of an hour, but The Queen and The Duke are reported to have chatted affectionately. The Duke's doctor remarked that as The Queen left The Duke's room there were tears in her eyes.

The King that never was lived an unfulfilled life. Appointed Governor of the Bahamas by Winston Churchill during the war, he subsequently held no other official role; instead, he and his Duchess lived out their lives in regal and extravagant splendour among Paris society, and

The Duchess – with her designer jewellery, her pugs and her haute couture gowns – became a fashion icon of the 1940s and 1950s. Frequently regarded as having encouraged his abdication, recently discovered correspondence would suggest otherwise.

Lord Louis Mountbatten was, until the abdication, a close friend of the uncrowned King, but afterwards – to Edward's chagrin – his allegiance shifted to the future King George VI. Mountbatten had a distinguished naval career during the war, followed by the roles of last Viceroy of India in 1947 and Governor General of the Independent Union of India from 1947–8. He served as First Sea Lord from 1954–9 and was delighted when his nephew married the future Queen Elizabeth II.

There are those who criticize the 1st Earl Mountbatten of Burma for his egotism, his social climbing (though as a great-grandson of Queen Victoria he was pretty near the top of the tree), his manoeuvrings and machinations and his obsession with his lineage. Nevertheless, he was highly regarded by those who served under him during the war – particularly on the ill-fated destroyer HMS *Kelly* in 1940 – and throughout his life he inspired affection and loyalty among many. His death, at the age of 79, at the hands of the IRA while on holiday at his home in Ireland, engendered widespread condemnation, not least because of the other fatalities suffered in the bomb blast, which destroyed

Mountbatten's boat, *Shadow V*. Mountbatten's grandson, Nicholas Knatchbull, and local lad Paul Maxwell also died in the blast, and the dowager Lady Brabourne died the following day.

The feelings of The Queen, and of The Prince of Wales – always close to his 'honorary grandfather' – can only be imagined. He was, said the Archbishop of Canterbury Dr Donald Coggan, "so rare a person".

Mountbatten was given a state funeral on 5 September 1979 – the order of which he had planned himself. His own horse Dolly was led at the front of the parade with her master's boots, by tradition, reversed in her stirrups.

MAUNDY MONEY

King George VI undertook it on a few occasions, but the ceremony of the Royal Maundy is something that The Queen has personally revived, distributing 'Maundy money' to her subjects in all but four years of her reign.

The day before Good Friday is Maundy Thursday, when, at the Last Supper, Christ washed the feet of his disciples and gave them the command or 'mandatum' (hence 'Maundy') to 'love one another'.

The present ceremony of the Royal Maundy dates from the thirteenth century but has altered somewhat over the

A day of celebration, the royal wedding really did seem like the stuff of fairytales, and gave a war-weary population something to cheer about.

Although the responsibilities demanded of Elizabeth made traditional family life difficult, there were still plenty of happy times.

The coronation was
attended by a crowd
of 7,500 dignitaries,
politicians and
notable peers.

It was a cause for nationwide
celebration, with millions joining
in any way they could.

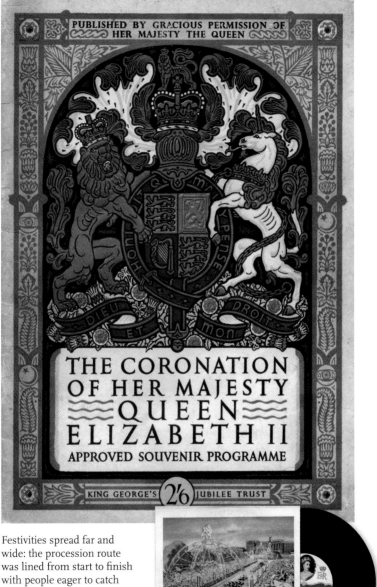

THE CORONATION OF HER MAJESTY QUEEN ELIZABETH II

APPROVED SOUVENIR PROGRAMME

KING GEORGE'S **2/6** JUBILEE TRUST

Festivities spread far and wide: the procession route was lined from start to finish with people eager to catch even the briefest glimpse.

CORONATION DAY

2nd JUNE 1953   LONG PLAY

All aspects of the royal family's life are the subject of public interest, right down to the famous corgis.

Her Majesty riding sidesaddle in the uniform of the Grenadier Guards. From parades to a day at the races, The Queen's love of horses is quite evident.

Prince Charles married Lady Diana
Spencer to scenes of jubilation on
29 July 1981.

A military inspection – just one part of Her Majesty's role in the forces.

Five days after Diana's tragic death, The Queen and Prince Philip view floral tributes outside the gates of Buckingham Palace.

The Queen Mother shares a joke with Prince Charles during a pageant to celebrate her 100th birthday.

Thousands flooded The Mall to honour The Queen's Golden Jubilee, marking 50 years on the throne.

TO CELEBRATE THE 50th ANNIVERSARY OF THE CORONATION

JUNE 2nd 1953

2003

HER MAJESTY QUEEN ELIZABETH II

The wedding of Prince William and Catherine Middleton – a thoroughly modern royal celebration.

For well over half a century, The Queen has shown an unerring sense of duty to her people.

years. Queen Elizabeth I only washed feet after they had already been washed; Charles I and Charles II avoided any foot washing for fear of contracting the plague, and after James II the foot washing was abandoned altogether and replaced with a cash gift. King George V managed just a one-off appearance in 1932.

The ceremony takes place in a different cathedral or abbey each year with one man and one woman for every year of the sovereign's life receiving a purse containing specially minted coins – one coin for each year of the sovereign's life. The recipients are chosen for their contribution to the local community rather than for their poverty (though recipients have been known to sell their sets for in excess of £100).

In 2011, at Westminster Abbey (where The Queen also distributed her first Maundy money in 1952), each man and woman received 85p in Maundy coins in a white purse and a £5 coin and 50p piece in a red purse. Traditionally struck in sterling silver, the coins bear the same image of The Queen's head – sculpted by Mary Gillick – as the coins of her coronation year (the image of The Queen's head on everyday currency has been changed three times).

The Maundy money is carried in procession on gold dishes that are carried on the heads of the Yeomen of the Guard in their Tudor uniforms. The Queen's attendants still carry towels as a reminder of the foot-washing tradition, and other attendants carry aromatic herbs, meant to ward off infection in medieval times. After a short service The Queen distributes the purses as the cathedral choir sings.

THE IRON LADY

It was in 1979 that Britain acquired its first woman prime minister in the shape of Margaret Hilda Thatcher. Born in Grantham, Lincolnshire in 1925, the daughter of a shop-keeper, Margaret Roberts was brought up as a monarchist in a working-class family. An academic high-flyer, after reading chemistry at Somerville College, Oxford she worked as a research chemist, but her interest in politics (she was president of the Oxford University Conservative Association) resulted in a change of direction. In 1951 she was approved as a Conservative candidate and in the same year married the wealthy divorced businessman Denis Thatcher, who supported his wife through thick and thin until his death in 2003. Their twins Mark and Carol were born in 1953, the same year that Margaret was called to the bar. Her parliamentary career began in 1959 when she became MP for Finchley – a constituency she represented until 1992.

Mrs Thatcher was an early champion of women's causes, having written a newspaper article at the time of The Queen's accession declaring that "a new era for women will be at hand". With the Sex Discrimination Act coming into force four years before she became prime minister, Mrs T, as she was nationally known, was well placed to prove the wisdom of her prophecy. She was Education Secretary from 1970–4, and elected Leader of the Opposition, defeating Edward Heath, in 1975.

Stubborn and opinionated, inflexible and autocratic and lacking any sense of humour were just some of the accusations levelled against the woman who was "not for turning" and who enjoyed a personal triumph in the successful outcome of the Falklands War (see also page 199). She was regarded by the Left as a leader who promoted capitalism and the accumulation of personal wealth at the expense of the downtrodden and unfortunate, but others saw her as just the shot in the arm that Britain needed at a time when the Empire was no more, the economy in dire straits and our influence on the world's stage was diminishing. In the Tory party she was, it was generally considered, 'the best man for the job'. Along with Ronald Reagan and Mikhail Gorbachev she presided over the fall of the Berlin wall and the improvement of international relations with Russia and the United States.

During the Falklands conflict Mrs Thatcher asked The Queen if Prince Andrew, a naval helicopter pilot who was determined to participate, should be allowed to do so. The Queen agreed and as a result The Prince saw active service, flying helicopter missions from HMS *Invincible*.

The British task force recaptured the islands in June 1982 after a battle lasting 74 days, during which 255 servicemen lost their lives. Mrs Thatcher, whose popularity before the war had been waning, called an election in June 1983 and secured a resounding victory.

Thatcher's firm stance with the unions, and her fighting of Britain's corner when it came to international relations – especially with Russia – resulted in the sobriquet 'The Iron Lady'.

But her popularity was not universal. In October 1984 the IRA planted a bomb in the Grand Hotel, Brighton, with the intention of killing the premier. It failed, though five others died in the blast. The Queen, enjoying a visit to Kentucky, USA, at the time, telephoned the prime minister to offer her condolences.

Margaret Thatcher held the office of prime minister from 1979–90, having successfully won a third term in 1987. Eventually her unpopular imposition of the poll tax (reshaped as the community charge), and an attitude to the European Community at odds with that of her cabinet, resulted in a challenge to her leadership by Michael Heseltine. To her bitter regret, Thatcher was ousted from the leadership, to be replaced, not by Heseltine, but by her former Chancellor of the Exchequer, John Major. Her departure from No. 10 was one of the rare occasions when the British people saw her evince any kind of emotion –

there were tears in her eyes as the Jaguar purred out of Downing Street with The Iron Lady in the back seat, alongside her loyal husband, who had little time for those who had brought about her downfall.

The Queen was respectful of her female premier, knowing from personal experience the problems of being a woman in a man's world on the international political stage. But there are amusing stories of their encounters. My favourite is one of little consequence, but which is nevertheless telling. Before one of the Tuesday evening audiences which the prime minister has with his/her sovereign around 25 times a year, and at which all matters of state – and other items of interest – are discussed, Mrs Thatcher's private secretary rang up The Queen's private secretary to inquire what Her Majesty would be wearing, so that the two did not clash.

"Oh, don't worry about that," said The Queen's private secretary. "Her Majesty never notices what anybody else is wearing."

"My grandfather couldn't have known what was in store for his grandchildren; yet his faith in the future gave him a quiet confidence that the stern tests would be overcome. And so it has proved. My father watched his grandchildren take their first steps and he knew all the sacrifices and anxiety of the dark days of the war had been worthwhile.

"Now it is our turn to work for a future which our grandchildren will step into one day. We cannot be certain what lies ahead for them but we should know enough to put them on the right path."

THE QUEEN'S CHRISTMAS MESSAGE, 1978

THE 1980s

"As I go about the country and abroad I meet many people who, all in their own ways, are making a real contribution to their community. I come across examples of unselfish service in all walks of life and in many unexpected places. Some people choose their occupation so that they can spend their lives in the service of their fellow citizens. Others find ways to give service in their spare time, through voluntary organizations or simply on their own individual initiative, contributing in a thousand ways to all that is best in our society.

"I want to say a word of thanks. And I include all those who don't realize they deserve thanks and are content that what they do is unseen and unrewarded. The very act of living a decent and upright life is in itself a positive factor in maintaining civilized standards."

THE QUEEN'S CHRISTMAS MESSAGE, 1980

The British monarchy is the oldest in Europe, dating back over a thousand years. Since we no longer live in a feudal society, when ruling with a rod of iron, invading new territory and appropriating property are the order of the day, there is no precise job specification. The monarch is, to put it simply, the titular custodian of the country's tradition and heritage but, equally important, the sovereign is a focus for national unity.

A LIFE OF SERVICE

The word which crops up more than any other in relation to the monarchy is 'duty' – the duty as head of state (the constitutional role which involves such things as appointing prime ministers, dissolving and opening Parliament, and making state visits to heads of other countries) and the duty as head of nation (the human side, which includes royal visits, launching ships, garden parties, cutting ribbons and

IN THE 1980s

Prime minister	Margaret Thatcher (1979–90)
Price of a pint of milk	17p
Price of a loaf of bread	37p
Price of a dozen eggs	72p
Price of petrol	99.8p per gallon; 44.4p per litre
Average weekly wage	£225
Average house price	£31,100
On TV	Breakfast Time; Dallas; Wogan; Spitting Image; Brideshead Revisited; Yes, Minister; EastEnders; Lovejoy; Casualty; Only Fools and Horses

opening hospitals). These duties are undertaken both in Britain and in the Commonwealth, where The Queen is also head of state.

What this rather bald job description does not take into account is the effect that meeting The Queen can have on her subjects. She and her family are, for want of a better description, in the 'happiness business'. On visits to hospitals and hospices, to the victims of national disasters and at events such as investitures The Queen provides a unique seal of approval, and it gives her a quality that no other leader could possibly emulate.

THE ROYAL YEAR

The one thing that becomes rapidly apparent is that The Queen's diary needs to be planned well in advance. For reasons of logistics and in order to provide some kind of structure to the year (and, one suspects, in order to preserve the sanity of a person whose entire life is mapped out), there is a distinctive pattern and rhythm to The Queen's year, as there has been for most of her predecessors. Though not immovable, the pattern tends to run thus:

January   Most of the month is spent at The Queen's private residence at Sandringham in Norfolk. King George VI died here on 6 February 1952 and that is why The Queen remains here until that date – the date of her accession.

February   The most usual time for overseas tours.

March	At work in Buckingham Palace from Monday to Friday with weekends at Windsor Castle.
April	Easter at Windsor.
May	At Windsor for the Royal Horse Show when there are house parties for family and close friends, then back to work at Buckingham Palace, with a visit to the Chelsea Flower Show towards the end of the month.
June	Visit to the Derby at Epsom; the Sovereign's 'Official' Birthday Parade – Trooping the Colour – on Horse Guards Parade; Ascot week is spent at Windsor.
July	Garden parties at Buckingham Palace and Holyroodhouse in Scotland.
August and September	Holidaying at Balmoral in Scotland for six weeks, often with other members of the royal family; the prime minister also makes a brief visit.
October	An overseas visit.

November	The State Opening of Parliament; the Festival of Remembrance at the Royal Albert Hall and the Remembrance Ceremony at the Cenotaph in Whitehall.
December	The latter part of the month at Sandringham for Christmas where close members of the family will gather and the Christmas Message is recorded.

From this calendar it could be assumed that The Queen takes a lot of holidays. That is far from being the case. There are *always* the red boxes to attend to and always a private secretary on duty to deal with the unending official demands on her time on matters connected with Britain and all the other Commonwealth countries.

REMEMBRANCE DAY CEREMONY

The Cenotaph on Whitehall, designed by Sir Edwin Lutyens and erected after the First World War to commemorate the fallen, is the focus for the annual service of remembrance of those who lost their lives not only in the two World Wars but also in subsequent conflicts, such as those in the Falklands, Bosnia, Iraq and Afghanistan. (The word 'cenotaph' means 'empty tomb'.)

A solemn occasion, the two minutes' silence is a time for reflection.

On the Sunday nearest the eleventh day of the eleventh month, The Queen leads the nation's tribute to those who gave their lives for their country. There is a gathering at the Cenotaph of around 10,000 servicemen and women and the ceremony is watched by thousands more civilians, and millions on television. At 11 a.m. a single cannon shot is fired to signal the start of two minutes' silence; a second shot follows to end it. Wreaths are laid by The Queen, other members of the royal family as heads of regiments, the prime minister and leaders of the main political parties, as well as ambassadors of Commonwealth countries and heads of the armed forces. A religious service is followed by a march past to the accompaniment of military bands.

THE STATE OPENING
OF PARLIAMENT

Unless there has been a general election, in which case it may be delayed, the State Opening of Parliament takes place in November each year. The Queen makes her way to Parliament by horse-drawn carriage, attended by liveried coachmen. To a fanfare of trumpets The Queen walks in procession with the uniformed Duke of Edinburgh to the throne in the House of Lords, from whence she summons the elected representatives of the people (the MPs) from the House of Commons. Her own representative, Black Rod, is despatched to the door of the Lower House where, by tradition, the door is slammed shut in his face – to demonstrate the independence of the elected house. He will strike his rod upon the door three times, whereupon it will be opened and he will summon the MPs to attend Her Majesty by saying: "Mr Speaker, The Queen commands this honourable House to attend Her Majesty immediately in the House of Peers." When both houses are assembled, The Queen announces her government's plans for the year ahead. Although The Queen may read it, the speech has been written for her by the government. At its conclusion she will say: "My Lords and Members of the House of Commons, I pray that the blessing of Almighty God may rest upon your counsels."

To be on the safe side, the cellars beneath the Houses of Parliament are searched with lanterns before every State Opening of Parliament by The Queen's Body Guard of the Yeomen of the Guard, as they have been since 1605 when Guy Fawkes tried to blow up the Houses of Parliament. Today more elaborate security measures are also in place. As an added precaution, an MP (usually from the Whips Office) is held hostage in the palace until The Queen returns. Just to be on the safe side …

TROOPING THE COLOUR

The Queen is commander-in-chief of all the armed forces, and Trooping the Colour (not *the* Trooping *of* the Colour) celebrates her official birthday, which is why it is also known as the Birthday Parade. (Aside from her real birthday on 21 April, The Queen has an official birthday which is celebrated on the first, second or (rarely) third Saturday in June. It is a tradition begun by Edward VII – whose own birthday was in November – since the weather is likely to be more reliable at that time.) The monarch's official birthday is celebrated at different times in different Commonwealth countries to suit their own conditions and traditions.

Trooping the Colour has its origins in the seventeenth century, but has been celebrated in more or less its current form since the reign of George IV. These days, The Queen joins the parade and reviews her troops in an open carriage pulled by a pair of Windsor greys; she has done so since her favourite horse Burmese retired in 1986, but before that she rode sidesaddle.

The carriage – a phaeton – will take her to Horse Guards Parade where, on the stroke of 11, The Queen reviews the Household Division both from the carriage and from her seat on a throne-like chair elevated on a dais. The 'colour' trooped is a standard from one of The Queen's regiments – a different one being chosen each year.

HOSTING STATE VISITS

Apart from making state visits to other countries herself, The Queen also hosts state visits from other heads of state to Britain at a rate of two or three a year. It is the government who suggest which leaders should be invited, and the visit will generally start on a Tuesday and end on a Friday (though more recently visits have been reduced to three days).

The visiting head of state will be met at Heathrow airport by The Prince of Wales who will travel with them to London where there will be a short carriage procession to Buckingham Palace.

At Buckingham Palace a lunch will follow and in the afternoon the visitor might meet another member of the royal family or lay a wreath on the Tomb of the Unknown Soldier in Westminster Abbey as a mark of respect. In the evening a state banquet will be held where the visiting head of state will be the guest of honour.

Such state banquets are glittering affairs when the royal plate, crystal and china are brought out – to be arranged with precision by the palace staff. The Queen will make a visit during the afternoon to check that everything is in place.

The following day involves a reception for high commissioners and the relevant ambassador, before the visiting head of state goes on to 10 Downing Street for talks and lunch with the prime minister.

Day three offers an opportunity to travel to places of special interest, and in the evening the head of state will host a banquet – usually at the residence of the relevant ambassador – for The Queen and The Duke of Edinburgh.

On Friday the visiting guests will leave the palace (where they will have been staying) at 10 a.m., accompanied by the Lord Chamberlain (the head of The Queen's household) who will see them off at the airport.

ROYAL VISITS AND ENGAGEMENTS

In addition to around 100 overseas engagements during the course of the year, The Queen will undertake 400 official engagements in the UK. Several hundred requests for The Queen's attendance are made each year, all of which are considered at 'diary meetings' in March and November and a shortlist put together to ensure that as much of the country is covered as possible and that the best use is made of The Queen's time.

In advance of the visit, The Queen's staff will have carried out a detailed recce of the proposed venues to make sure that security is in place, to confirm the order of events and the content and to ensure that the visit is likely to run smoothly.

The hosts will be advised in advance of the protocol involved – how The Queen is greeted (a bow from the neck for men, a brief bob from the women – though in many instances nowadays there has been a relaxation of these niceties) along with such things as the presentation of flowers (posies are preferred to bouquets).

In addition to The Queen, 13 other members of the royal family perform official duties and in the course of a year, half a million people will have had a brief encounter with royalty.

THE YEOMEN OF THE GUARD

The Royal Body Guard of the Yeomen of the Guard are The Queen's official bodyguards and they come under the responsibility of the Lord Chamberlain's office. ('The Beef-eaters' is the nickname of the Yeoman warders at the Tower of London – an entirely different corps who just happen to have a similar uniform.)

Their headquarters are at St James's Palace and they are the oldest military corps in the world, dating back to the reign of Henry VII in 1485. Their uniform has altered little since that time: a scarlet doublet patterned in red and gold with the sovereign's cipher on the chest – EIIR, white ruff, white gloves, black velvet hat trimmed with red, white and blue rosettes, black shoes with large gold buckles and red hose. They are armed with swords and each carries a 7-ft halberd or 'partisan'.

THE GENTLEMEN-AT-ARMS

The Gentlemen-at-Arms are more senior military attendants of the sovereign – created during the sixteenth century – comprising five officers and 27 gentlemen. They wear the uniform of a Heavy Dragoon Guards officer of the 1820s – their helmets are topped with cascades of white-feathered plumes – and they are on duty at all state occasions, rather like the Yeomen of the Guard.

THE ROYAL COMPANY OF ARCHERS

The sovereign's protection in Scotland is looked after by the Royal Company of Archers, formed in 1676 by an act of the Privy Council of Scotland. There are 500 of them and, like the Yeomen of the Guard, they come under the responsibility of the Lord Chamberlain's office. All well-connected Scots, they provide their own uniform – a dark green tunic with a matching kilt and Balmoral bonnet – and like their English counterparts they act as The Queen's personal bodyguard on official occasions north of the border.

KEY EVENTS IN THE 1980s ∞∞∞∞∞∞∞∞∞∞∞∞∞∞∞

1980   Steelworkers go on strike from January to April – the
        industry is one of those most badly hit by the recession:
        11,000 jobs are threatened. Mrs Thatcher gets tough
        on government spending, on Europe – winning a big
        cut in Britain's payments to the EC – and on policy
        reversals – "You turn if you want to; the lady's not for
        turning." As a result a new word enters the English
        language – 'handbagging.'

1981   A miners' strike is threatened but Mrs Thatcher
        offers them more money in an attempt to avert
        industrial action.

        Arthur Scargill is elected president of the National
        Union of Mineworkers.

        Half of all women now go out to work as against one
        in five in 1951. The first women take part in the Oxford
        and Cambridge University Boat Race – Sue Brown, the
        cox, steers the Oxford crew to victory.

1982   Unemployment tops 3 million.

        Laker Airways and DeLorean cars (the ones with the
        gull-wing doors) fail.

        Channel 4 opens and video recorders start to appear.

From April to July the Falklands War rages.

1983 Unemployment reaches 3.75 million.

Women anti-nuclear protestors set up camp outside the Greenham Common airbase.

1984 National miners' strike begins in March in response to pit closures and a 5.2 per cent pay increase. Nottinghamshire miners – against the strike –break away and form their own union, the Union of Democratic Mineworkers. Violence breaks out on picket lines. Arthur Scargill is at loggerheads with the coal board chairman Ian McGregor who is attempting to close 20 pits with 20,000 job losses. The strike runs on but by November over 800 miners have returned to work.

Early-morning television begins with Breakfast Time on BBC1 hosted by Frank Bough and Selina Scott; ITV follows a month later with TV-AM.

Margaret Thatcher returns to office for a second term.

Scientists at the University of East Anglia warn of the 'greenhouse effect' due to carbon dioxide build-up caused by the burning of fossil fuels.

1985 Half the miners are back, the other half still on strike.

The Sinclair C5 battery and pedal-powered tricycle is launched in January; it has a range of 20 miles and costs £399. Its inventor Sir Clive Sinclair predicts the demise of the petrol-powered engine by the end of the century. In October Sinclair calls in the official receiver.

Compact disc players become popular.

1986 Production of the *Sunday Times* and *News of the World* moves to Rupert Murdoch's highly automated plant at Wapping.

There is a police clash with pickets over job losses.

Britain and France agree to the creation of the Channel Tunnel after 200 years of false starts.

1987 The picketing at Wapping is called off after a year of often violent confrontation between print workers and police.

Black Monday wipes £50 billion off the value of shares – nearly twice that of the Wall Street crash of 1929. (It is blamed partly on USA's rising interest rates and trade deficits and partly on the start of computerized dealing which began in 1986.)

Mary Whitehouse launches an attack on the bad language in EastEnders.

One of Prince Edward's first media ventures after leaving the Royal Marines is a royal version of the TV game show *It's a Knockout*. The show raised £1 million for charity but made rather uncomfortable viewing.

The ozone layer is a cause of concern. Seventy nations pledge to do their bit in stopping the use of chlorofluorocarbons used as propellants in aerosol cans, fridges and air-conditioning units.

The Church of England gives the go-ahead for women to be ordained as priests.

Margaret Thatcher is elected for a third term.

"Last July we had the joy of seeing our eldest son married amid scenes of great happiness, which made 1981 a very special year for us. The wonderful response the wedding evoked was very moving."

THE QUEEN'S CHRISTMAS MESSAGE, 1981

CHARLES AND DIANA

It is easy to forget, now, with the benefit of hindsight and with knowledge of the outcome, just how buoyed up was the entire world by the marriage of Charles, Prince of Wales, to Lady Diana Spencer. The Queen's own sentiments were shared by the vast majority of her subjects.

Regarded for years as 'the world's most eligible bachelor', Charles had been romantically linked with a number of women including a model, an actress, the rather more suitable daughter of The Duke of Wellington, and Camilla Shand, who went on to marry Andrew Parker Bowles, the ex-boyfriend of Princess Anne. Media speculation was unceasing: The Prince was past 30, he was the heir to the throne; it was time he got married and ensured the succession.

Charles's 'honorary grandfather', Lord Louis Mountbatten, famously advised him, "a man should sow his wild oats and have as many affairs as he can before settling down, but for a wife he should choose a suitable, attractive and sweet-charactered girl before she met anyone else she might fall for".

Diana Frances Spencer, born on 1 July 1961, third child of the Viscount and Viscountess Althorp, fitted the bill perfectly. At the time of their wedding, Charles was 32, she was 20. They had known each other, however slightly, for some time (he had dated her older sister), and the Spencer family was known to the royals – Diana's father had served as equerry to both King George VI and The Queen, and her grandmother Ruth, Lady Fermoy, was a lady-in-waiting to Queen Elizabeth The Queen Mother.

In the summer of 1980 Diana was working at a Kensington kindergarten and shared a flat with several other 'Sloaney' girls. Charles proposed in February 1981, and the shy, attractive but slightly awkward 'Lady Di' became an instant hit with the media.

The couple were married at St Paul's Cathedral on 29 July 1981, chosen in preference to the more usual Westminster Abbey because of its ability to accommodate more guests and because of its architectural beauty – this was to be the fairytale wedding to end all fairytale weddings.

The day of the wedding was a national holiday. Three-quarters of a billion people around the world watched on television as the bride travelled in the Glass Coach with her father from Clarence House (where she had been staying) to St Paul's. Enveloped in a crinoline-like confection of rumpled ivory taffeta designed by David and Elizabeth Emmanuel, Diana Spencer married her Prince and became the first Princess of Wales for 71 years.

The Prince and Princess's children were born soon after the wedding: Prince William Arthur Philip Louis on 21 June 1982 and Prince Henry Charles Albert David – to be known as 'Harry' – on 15 September 1984.

The couple made their homes at Highgrove in Gloucestershire and Kensington Palace.

THE FALKLANDS WAR

The small group of islands in the South Atlantic Ocean – beyond the tip of South America – were no more than a name to most of us and the sum total of our knowledge prior to the events of the 1980s was probably that they were cold, windy and home to penguins. Even politicians were uncertain as to their precise location on the map. But when Argentina invaded the islands they called *Islas Malvinas*, and to which they had laid claim only briefly prior to British rule in 1833, British forces were sent by Margaret Thatcher to reclaim an overseas territory that had been under British jurisdiction since the late seventeenth century.

The Falkland Islands were invaded at the behest of the Argentine Junta (military-led government) on 2 April 1982 when the inhabitants of the capital, Port Stanley, were rounded up and held at gunpoint in a hall. The following day the Argentines occupied the neighbouring island of South Georgia and on 5 April HMS *Invincible* and HMS *Hermes* set sail from Portsmouth.

Prince Andrew served as a helicopter pilot on HMS *Invincible* and was among those charged with attempting to deflect missile attacks on British warships. It had been suggested that The Queen might want her son exempted from active service, but this was categorically refuted when it was announced, "There is no question in her mind that he should go"

By mid-April Britain was wholeheartedly behind 'The Iron Lady' as she reasserted the nation's claim to one of her sovereign territories – however small and distant it may be. Those who lived there had friends and relations in the UK and suddenly this distant outpost symbolized Britain's tenacity and determination in the face of bully-boy tactics.

On 13 June the British forces attacked Mount Tumbledown and Wireless Ridge and a day later fighting ended as the British re-took Port Stanley. The Argentine Commander, Major General Mario Menendez, surrendered to the British Land Forces Commander, Major General Jeremy Moore who sent a signal to London: "The Falkland Islands are once more under the government desired by their inhabitants. God save The Queen." However, it was not until 13 July that the Argentine Junta, under their president, General Galtieri, accepted an end to hostilities.

The Prince of Wales welcomed back *Canberra* as she returned to Southampton with British servicemen on 11 July.

The prime minister's popularity – on the wane after only three years in office – received an incalculable boost, and it was she, rather than The Queen, who oversaw the march past of the returning troops. Mrs Thatcher had a very good war.

"In the year I was born, radio communication was barely out of its infancy; there was no television; civil aviation had hardly started and space satellites were still in the realm of science fiction. When my grandfather visited India in 1911, it took three weeks by sea to get there. Last month I flew back from Delhi to London in a matter of hours. It took King George V three months to make the round trip. Travel and communication have entered a completely new dimension.

"Yet in spite of these advances the age-old problems of human communication are still with us. We have the means of sending and receiving messages, we can travel to meetings in distant parts of the world, we can exchange experts; but we still have difficulty in finding the right messages to send, we can still ignore the messages we don't like to hear and we can still talk in riddles and listen without trying to comprehend.

"Perhaps even more serious is the risk that this mastery of technology may blind us to the more fundamental needs of people. Electronics cannot create comradeship; computers cannot generate compassion; satellites cannot transmit tolerance."

THE QUEEN'S CHRISTMAS MESSAGE, 1983

THE DAWN OF THE ELECTRONICS ERA

1954   The 'Electronic Brain' for office use is announced by IBM. Available to rent for £25,000 per month; 30 are ordered.

1956   'ERNIE' – the 'Electronic Random Number Indicating Equipment' enables the launch of Premium Bonds.

1957   Russians are the first into space with Sputnik 1. The Russian dog Laika is sent into space a month later but does not come back.

1958   The Queen makes the first STD (Subscriber Trunk Dialling) call to launch the new system, dialling Edinburgh direct from Bristol without having to 'go through the operator'.

1959   The pace quickens – monkeys survive a space flight.

A Soviet rocket hits the Moon and the Russians photograph its 'dark side'.

The first transistor radios appear on sale – still pretty hefty compared to those of today.

1960   Britain announces it is to fund a supersonic aircraft capable of reaching 2,000 m.p.h. at a cost of £5-6 million each. (Concorde would make her maiden flight 19 years later.)

1962   Telstar satellite relays the first TV pictures from the
       USA to the UK: the start of worldwide television.

1972   Clive Sinclair launches the first pocket calculator – the
       Sinclair Executive – which runs off four hearing-aid
       batteries that drive a silicon chip.

1973   Motorola makes the first fully mobile phone.

1975   Mainframe computers are starting to become more widely
       used in business – each occupies an entire room. They
       are staffed by white-coated workers since the air has to
       be dust free. (Each of these monsters had about the same
       computing power as one of today's pocket calculators.)

1982   Home computers – led by the Sinclair ZX priced at
       £100 – are becoming commonplace.

1984   Vodaphone makes the first call on a first-generation
       cellular phone in the UK on 1 January.

1986   Big Bang Day – the Stock Exchange starts computerized
       dealing but the system fails (briefly). Deregulation
       of the financial markets leads to an increase in the
       number of banks and brokerage firms setting up
       business in Britain.

       The 'Yuppy' (young, upwardly mobile professional
       earning a huge salary) is born.

"The happy arrival of our fourth grandchild gave great cause for family celebrations. But for parents and grandparents, a birth is also a time for reflection on what the future holds for the baby and how they can best ensure its safety and happiness. To do that, I believe we must be prepared to learn as much from them as they do from us. We could use some of that sturdy confidence and devastating honesty with which children rescue us from self-doubts and self-delusions. We could borrow that unstinting trust of the child in its parents for our dealings with each other. Above all, we must retain the child's readiness to forgive, with which we are all born and which it is all too easy to lose as we grow older."

THE QUEEN'S CHRISTMAS MESSAGE, 1984

THE QUEEN AS MOTHER, GRANDMOTHER AND GREAT-GRANDMOTHER

It was while Elizabeth and Philip were in Kenya, undertaking a tour on behalf of the King, that George VI died and Elizabeth became Queen. The role of wife and mother and heir to the throne was now added to by that of sovereign.

From the very beginning there were separations from her children: the post Coronation tour from November 1953 to May 1954 was the most arduous of all, and The Queen's longest. While the effect this absence had on the children is often discussed, The Queen's own feelings on being apart from her children must also be considered. She had always wanted a large family, and her desire to protect her children's privacy in their early years was evident in her Christmas message of 1958 when she said: "We believe that public life is not a fair burden to place on children."

Prince Andrew was born in 1960 and Prince Edward in 1964. Now established in her role, The Queen could afford a little more time for her children, though she was reported to be sitting up in bed reading through the contents of her red boxes within a few hours of Prince Andrew being born.

By all accounts The Queen particularly enjoyed the evenings when the children's nanny was off duty and she could bath and put her young sons to bed herself. She taught them their alphabet, got up to attend to them if they had a fretful night, and generally found time to be a much more 'hands-on' parent than she had done with her first two children.

Life has changed for all families over the last 60 years, and The Queen's own attitude to life has changed with that of her subjects. From the days when children were 'seen and not heard' – a dictum in many houses across the land in the first half of the twentieth century, not just in royal palaces – to these days, when the vast majority of parents are far more involved with the daily lives of their children, so is The Queen perhaps more at ease with her children – and grandchildren – than she has ever been. Since the death of Queen Elizabeth The Queen Mother and Princess Margaret, The Queen is not just the titular head of the family, but also its matriarch.

THE QUEEN'S CHRISTMAS CARDS

The Queen and The Duke of Edinburgh send out about 750 Christmas cards every year. There is a royal insignia on the outside, a family photograph on the inside right (more informal as the years have gone by) and a printed greeting and signature on the left-hand side. To close friends and family The Queen will sign herself Lilibet, to others Elizabeth, and some of the cards (those that are more official than intimate) may be signed Elizabeth R with an 'autopen' – a device that can duplicate The Queen's signature. Keen eyes can tell the real thing from the automated.

'TELEGRAMS FROM THE QUEEN'

The Anniversaries Office at Buckingham Palace sends out congratulatory cards (no longer telegrams) to those who reach the age of 100 – being informed by the Department of Work and Pensions. The tradition was started in 1917 by King George V. When Elizabeth II came to the throne there were 300 sent out each year; now there are around 4,500 in Britain and 2,200 in other parts of the realm. The card bears a photograph of The Queen and a printed signature, along with cordial greetings. At 105 another card will be sent, and then yearly thereafter. One venerable old lady complained that The Queen was wearing the same dress year after year on her birthday card. A new photograph was taken.

CONGRATULATORY CARDS

The Queen also sends cards to those couples celebrating their diamond wedding anniversary – 60 years. Due to the number of weddings that took place just after the war, 2005 was a bumper year for diamond weddings and the palace sent out 24,000 cards all over the world – 18,000 in Britain. Cards are also sent out on the occasion of 65th and 70th (platinum) anniversaries. Such cards can be applied for at: The Anniversaries Office, Buckingham Palace, London SW1A 1AA, or by phone.

LADIES-IN-WAITING AND EQUERRIES

When The Queen has a public duty she is accompanied by a lady-in-waiting (two or more on overseas trips). Appointed by The Queen herself, ladies-in-waiting tend to be personal friends. They serve as companions and assistants to The Queen – sitting next to her in the royal car and carrying any posies and gifts that are presented to her.

I was standing on the lawn at the back of Buckingham Palace at a garden party a few years ago, talking to two ladies-in-waiting. We all three watched as The Queen made her way among the people smiling and chatting. After a few moments one of the ladies-in-waiting sighed and said quite softly, "I'd do anything for that woman." It was not an idle comment. Their dedication to The Queen is unquestioning and impressive.

Inside Buckingham Palace the ladies-in-waiting have their own office where they handle much of The Queen's day-to-day correspondence. The Queen receives around 50,000 personal letters each year (including many inviting her to parties and weddings!) and if the year includes a special event the number can be nearer to 100,000. The ladies-in-waiting will sign thank-you letters on behalf of The Queen, and The Queen herself sifts through many of the letters sent in – regarding it as an important way of keeping in touch with the mood of the nation.

Equerries have different roles depending on which member of the royal family they work for. In Her Majesty's household the equerry looks after guests in the social sense – from prime ministers to family friends. The private secretary will manage the diary.

The term 'equerry' (with the emphasis on the second syllable – e-*querr*-ee) is derived from the French écurie, meaning 'stable' – an indication that the role, dating back to medieval times, once included the management of horses. Indeed, the Crown Equerry is in charge of the Royal Mews – the horses, carriages and cars that transport the sovereign and her family on state occasions.

"Looking at the morning newspapers, listening to the radio and watching television, it is only too easy to conclude that nothing is going right in the world. All this year we seem to have had nothing but bad news with a constant stream of reports of plane crashes, earthquakes, volcanic eruptions and famine – and as if natural disasters were not enough, we hear of riots, wars, acts of terrorism and generally of man's inhumanity to man. It used to be said that "no news is good news" but today you might think that "good news is no news". Yet there is a lot of good news and some wonderful things are going on in spite of the frightening headlines.

"I am in the fortunate position of being able to meet many of these people, for every year some two thousand come to investitures at Buckingham Palace to be honoured for acts of bravery or to be recognized for service to their fellow citizens. They come from all walks of life and they don't blow their own trumpets; so unless, like me, you are able to read the citations describing what they have done, you could not begin to guess at some of the remarkable stories that lie behind their visits to the palace."

THE QUEEN'S CHRISTMAS MESSAGE, 1985

THE HONOURS SYSTEM

The honours list is issued twice each year – on New Year's Day (though the honours are published in newspapers the day before) and on The Queen's Official Birthday in June.

Aside from diplomats, members of the armed forces and those who have served in government or the Civil Service, many recipients of honours have been recommended for

The granting of honours has been a part of
The Queen's duty since the earliest days of her reign.

their work within the community or for services to charity. Alongside entertainers and celebrities, actors and writers you will find doctors and nurses, lollipop and dinner ladies, road sweepers and gardeners.

Anyone may nominate a person for an honour and the names put forward are considered over 18 months. The

Prime Minister's Office makes the final choice, narrowing down an enormous list of suggestions to around 1,100 names on each list. Around six weeks before each honours list is published, the intended recipient will receive a letter from 10 Downing Street. The recipient must tick a box to indicate acceptance or refusal, and then sit back and wait for the list to be published. He or she must tell no one of the appointment.

Most honours are those of the Most Excellent Order of the British Empire, established in 1917 (which is why the orders carry the heads of King George V and Queen Mary). In ascending order of rank they are:

- Member (MBE)
- Officer (OBE)
- Commander (CBE)
- Knight or Dame Commander (KBE or DBE)
- Knight or Dame Grand Cross (GBE)

The Order of the Bath is awarded to members of the armed forces and occasionally to Civil Servants. The Order of St Michael and St George is awarded to diplomats.

THE ROYAL VICTORIAN ORDER

In the gift of the sovereign, the Royal Victorian Order was founded by Queen Victoria in 1896 and is awarded to those who have given distinguished service to The Queen and other members of the royal family – many of them members of the royal household or who serve the family in other ways at home and overseas.

The award is also made to members of the royal family. In ascending order of rank they are:

- Member of the Royal Victorian Order (MVO)
- Lieutenant of the Royal Victorian Order (LVO)
- Commander of the Royal Victorian Order (CVO)
- Knight/Dame Commander of the Royal Victorian Order (KCVO/DCVO)
- Knight/Dame Grand Cross of the Royal Victorian Order (GCVO)

INVESTITURES

Up to 20 investitures are held each year – usually at Buckingham Palace, but increasingly now at Windsor Castle. In Scotland they are held at The Palace of Holyroodhouse in Edinburgh. The recipient of an honour is allowed to bring three guests. The Queen, The Prince of Wales or, on rare occasions, The Princess Royal may present the awards and the dress code for recipients is uniform or morning dress (rarely lounge suits) for men, and smart day clothes for ladies.

A small hook is affixed to the left lapel or shoulder so that The Queen may simply hang the award in place; neck orders (CBE and Knighthood) are placed over the bowed head of the recipient.

While a military band plays light music (selections from the musicals are popular) the guests assemble. The national anthem marks the arrival of The Queen and the ceremony begins, with the Lord Chamberlain reading out the names of recipients and the reason for their honour: "For services to nursing in the West Midlands." Knighthoods are awarded first, with each recipient going down on one knee on a cushioned stool and The Queen smartly tapping each shoulder with a shining sword before placing the medal ribbon over their head. The ceremony continues in descending order of rank. Each recipient will receive a few words from The Queen and a question or two.

After the ceremony, The Queen leaves the ballroom and the families are reunited. It is a day that no one forgets, especially those who have heeded the words of the Comptroller of the Lord Chamberlain's Office during their briefing: "Please relax, because if you relax you will enjoy the ceremony and if you enjoy the ceremony you will remember it."

Few will ever relax, but hopefully all will remember it as one of the most special days of their lives.

THE ORDER OF THE GARTER

The highest order of chivalry, and the oldest, the Order of the Garter was created in 1348 and can be held by only 24 members in addition to the sovereign and The Prince of Wales at any one time. The Queen was invested as a Lady of the Garter on 11 November 1947 by her father, and eight days later he conferred the same honour upon her husband-to-be, Prince Philip.

On 17 June 1968 The Queen invested Prince Charles as a Knight of the Garter the year before he was invested as Prince of Wales. In 2011, Prince William was invested as the 1,000th member of the Order.

Members of the Order are suffixed KG, and the Garter Service – when new members of the Order are installed – is held in June each year at St George's Chapel, Windsor. The ceremony is one of great pageantry – the Knights process in their deep blue velvet Garter robes and black velvet hats decorated with white ostrich plumes. The patron saint of the Order is St George, and each member has around his or her neck a chain supporting a unique maquette of St George slaying the dragon.

THE ORDER OF THE THISTLE

Scotland's equivalent to the Order of the Garter is the Order of the Thistle. The number is limited to 16 men and women who have made an exceptional contribution to public life in Scotland. Holders of the Order wear green velvet robes and the 'thistle collar with badge appendant'. Like the Garter chain, it must be returned on the death of the holder. Holders are entitled to the suffix KT.

Both the Order of the Garter and the Order of the Thistle were opened up to women by The Queen in 1987. Women members of the orders are known as Lady Companions.

THE ORDER OF MERIT

Founded by King Edward VII at the time of his coronation in 1902, the Order of Merit (OM) is awarded to individuals who have made outstanding contributions in the fields of the arts, literature, learning and science. There are only 24 holders at any one time, plus a small number of overseas recipients. The order is an enamel cross bearing the simple words 'For Merit'.

THE ORDER OF COMPANIONS OF HONOUR

Instituted in 1917 by King George V for those who have contributed work of national importance, the Order of Companions of Honour (CH) is limited to the sovereign and 65 ordinary members (overseas recipients are admitted only as honorary members and may be recommended by Commonwealth leaders). The gold medal bears a representation of an oak tree and bears the motto: 'In action faithful and in honour clear.'

"Like everyone else I learn about what is going on in the world from the media, but I am fortunate to have another source of information. Every day hundreds of letters come to my desk, and I make a point of reading as many of them as I possibly can ...

I value all these letters for keeping me in touch with your views and opinions, but there are a few letters which reflect the darker side of human nature.

"It is only too easy for passionate loyalty to one's own country, race or religion, or even to one's favourite football club, to be corroded into intolerance, bigotry, and ultimately into violence."

THE QUEEN'S CHRISTMAS MESSAGE, 1987

THE PRIME MINISTERS

Aside from assiduously monitoring the media for her information on domestic and world affairs, and scrutinizing the contents of her red boxes (which contain briefings from overseas as well as the United Kingdom), The Queen also has weekly meetings with her prime minister – usually on Tuesday evenings at Buckingham Palace. No notes are taken, no recordings are made and no one else is present, and so it has been throughout The Queen's reign. They are, according to Sir John Major, 'incredibly relaxed and very wide ranging'.

All her prime ministers admit to having found her a wise and experienced sounding board on all manner of subjects.

Winston Churchill	1940–5; 1951–5 (Conservative)
Anthony Eden	1955–7 (Conservative)
Harold Macmillan	1957–63 (Conservative)
Alec Douglas-Home	1963–4 (Conservative)
Harold Wilson	1964–70 and 1974–6 (Labour)
Edward Heath	1970–4 (Conservative)
James Callaghan	1976–9 (Labour)

Margaret Thatcher	1979–1990 (Conservative)
John Major	1990–7 (Conservative)
Tony Blair	1997–2007 (Labour)
Gordon Brown	2007–10 (Labour)
David Cameron	2010 (Conservative–Liberal Democrat coalition)

PRINCE ANDREW AND SARAH FERGUSON

It was at Royal Ascot in the summer of 1985 that Prince Andrew began his relationship with the daughter of The Prince of Wales's polo manager, Major Ronald Ferguson. As with every royal son the media had watched and reported on his various liaisons with intense interest. Some were regarded as suitable, others less so – the actress Koo Stark had appeared topless in a film some years earlier and raised a few eyebrows. But the nation approved of the red-haired Sarah Ferguson – a bright and lively Hampshire girl who was seen as a good match for a popular Prince who had a distinguished service in the Falklands War as a helicopter pilot. They called her 'Fergie' and regarded her as a breath of fresh air. The couple married at Westminster Abbey on 23 July 1986 and on the day of their wedding The Prince was given the titles of Duke of York, Earl of Inverness and Baron Killyleagh by The Queen. The couple built their own home, not far from Windsor – Sunninghill Park – and went on to have two daughters: Princess Beatrice Elizabeth Mary of York was born on 8 August 1988 and Princess Eugenie Victoria Helena of York on 23 March 1990.

THE 1990s

"... it seems to me that there is one deep and overriding anxiety for us all on which we should reflect today. That is the threat of war in the Middle East. The servicemen in the Gulf who are spending Christmas at their posts under this threat are much in our thoughts. And there are many others, at home and abroad, servicemen and civilians, who are away from their own firesides. Wherever they are, may they all, when their duty is done, soon be reunited with their families safe and sound ...

"It is they and their kind who, by resisting the bully and the tyrant, ensure that we live in the sort of world in which we can celebrate this season safely with our families."

THE QUEEN'S CHRISTMAS MESSAGE, 1990

With wars in the Gulf and in Bosnia this was to be the first of two challenging decades for Britain's armed forces, and one of mixed emotions for The Queen. Conflicts both overseas and within her own family were to have far-reaching consequences. This was the decade of The Queen's annus horribilis: of the Windsor Castle fire, of the divorces of three of her children and of Princess Diana's death. But there was one event which must have given her some solace and gave the nation another reason to celebrate this remarkable woman – the golden wedding of The Queen and The Duke of Edinburgh.

THE QUEEN AS HEAD
OF THE ARMED FORCES

On enlistment into the services, men and women swear an oath of allegiance to The Queen – only the Royal Navy is exempt by tradition since it already stems from the royal prerogative, an 'exclusive right' to that sovereign.

IN THE 1990s

Prime minister	John Major (1990–7);
	Tony Blair (1997–2007)
Price of a pint of milk	31p
Price of a loaf of bread	65p
Price of a dozen eggs	£1.21
Price of petrol	273.4p per gallon; 60.8p per litre
Average weekly wage	£385
Average house price	£65,600
On TV	Inspector Morse;
	Changing Rooms;
	Who Wants to be a Millionaire?;
	Ground Force;
	The Darling Buds of May

As Head of the Armed Forces The Queen technically has the right to declare war, though in these days of a Constitutional Monarchy this is done only on the advice of ministers.

The Queen meets regularly with the Chief of the Defence Staff and the heads of all the armed services, and is kept informed of matters military by her Defence Services

Secretary – a serving officer who is a member of the royal household and her official link with the services.

All the senior members of the royal family have connections with the armed forces, and several of them have seen active service.

THE QUEEN

Princess Elizabeth joined the ATS (the Auxiliary Territorial Service) in 1945 and as such was the first female member of the royal family to become an active full-time member of the armed services. Today The Queen is Colonel-in-Chief of the five regiments that make up the Foot Guards (the Grenadier Guards, the Coldstream Guards, the Scots Guards, the Welsh Guards and the Irish Guards). The Queen was also Lord High Admiral until she appointed The Duke of Edinburgh to the role in 2011.

THE DUKE OF EDINBURGH

Prince Philip served in the Royal Navy from 1939–52 when The Queen's accession brought an end to what would have undoubtedly been a high-flying naval career. He was mentioned in despatches in 1941 (see also page 236) while in charge of a searchlight on HMS *Valiant* during night action in the Battle of Matapan. He was a lieutenant at the time of his engagement to Princess Elizabeth and rose to the rank of Commander when he left the service. He undertook Royal Air Force (RAF) flying instruction in 1952 and was presented with his Wings in 1953, the same year he was appointed Admiral of the Fleet. He holds the same rank in the New Zealand and Australian navies. He holds many high ranks in the services, including Marshal of the Royal Air Force, Captain General of the Royal Marines, Field Marshal of the British Army and, since 2011, Lord High Admiral.

THE PRINCE OF WALES

The Prince of Wales served in the Royal Navy and trained in the RAF. After RAF training during his second year at Cambridge, he went to the RAF College at Cranwell to train as a jet pilot and gained his Wings by passing the gruelling Parachute Regiment course. His naval career began at the Royal Naval College in Dartmouth. He went on to serve on the guided missile destroyer HMS *Norfolk* (1971–2), the frigate HMS *Minerva* (1972–3) and the frigate HMS *Jupiter* (1974). He qualified as a helicopter pilot at Royal Naval Air Station (RNAS) Yeovilton in 1974, then joined 845 Naval Air Squadron operating from HMS *Hermes*. His naval career culminated in him commanding the minesweeper HMS *Bronington* in 1976.

He holds the ranks of Admiral in the Royal Navy, general in the Army, Air Chief Marshal in the RAF and is Commodore-in-Chief, Plymouth.

The Prince is patron of a number of charities and organizations that help to look after the welfare of soldiers and their families, including the Airborne Forces Security Fund, the War Widows' Association of Great Britain, The British Forces Foundation, The Royal Naval Benevolent Trust and The White Ensign Association. The Prince has a special relationship with 12 regiments in this country and ten in the Commonwealth. It is rather more than a passive relationship, too. The Prince is kept informed of the activities of his regiments and is formally briefed on a regular basis. As Colonel-in-Chief or Royal Colonel The Prince often visits his regiments on bases in this country and abroad, meeting soldiers and their families, and he pays frequent visits to injured soldiers at their regimental bases and the Royal Centre for Defence Medicine at Selly Oak Hospital in Birmingham.

It is a little-known fact that injured personnel will often receive a letter with a bottle of whisky from The Prince to speed their recovery, and he always writes to the families of those servicemen in his regiments who have lost their lives on active service.

THE DUCHESS OF CORNWALL

The Duchess of Cornwall also has a close affinity with the military through her father's highly distinguished military career in the Second World War for which he was awarded two Military Crosses. Her Royal Highness is patron and an honorary member of the Desert Rats Association as well as being Royal Colonel of the 4th Battalion The Rifles, Commodore-in-Chief of Naval Medical Services, Royal Navy, Sponsor of HMS *Astute* and Honorary Commodore of both RAF Leeming and RAF Halton. In 2011 The Duchess became Colonel-in-Chief of The Queen's Own Rifles of Canada.

THE DUKE OF YORK

Prince Andrew joined the Royal Navy in 1979 on a short service commission, attending the Royal Naval College at Dartmouth and winning his 'Green Beret' with the Royal Marines before passing out of Dartmouth and undertaking flying training with the RAF and the Royal Navy. Awarded his Wings in 1981, he was also named 'best pilot' in the group and became an accomplished handler of both the Gazelle and Sea King helicopters. After operational flying training his first front-line unit was 820 Naval Air Squadron, and six months later The Prince found himself on active service as part of the Task Force that sailed to the Falkland Islands on board HMS *Invincible*. In the Falklands War The Prince took part in various missions including anti-submarine warfare and anti-surface warfare search, as well as search and air rescue. On his return he trained to fly Lynx helicopters, was promoted to Lieutenant and appointed by The Queen as a personal aide-de-camp.

The Prince remained in the Royal Navy, serving on HMS *Brazen*, HMS *Edinburgh* and becoming Flight Commander 829 NAS. In 1992 he was appointed to the Army Command and Staff Course at the Staff College, Camberley and promoted to Lieutenant Commander. He commanded the minehunter HMS *Cottesmore* from 1993–4.

Posts at the Ministry of Defence and the Diplomacy Section of the Royal Navy followed, along with promotion to the rank of Commander in 1999.

The Duke of York left the Royal Navy in 2001 and was promoted to Honorary Captain in 2005. He is Commodore-in-Chief of the Fleet Air Arm.

After leaving the navy he undertook the role of trade envoy to the United Kingdom. It was a controversial role that he relinquished in 2011. His detractors dubbed him 'Air-Miles Andy', but there are many in industry and business who regard his achievements – unseen and largely ignored by the journalists who snipe at his apparent jet-set lifestyle – as effective and highly commendable. A glance at the Court Circular during his years as trade envoy reveal a capacity for attending business appointments and delegations overseas that few would envy.

THE EARL OF WESSEX

Prince Edward spent three years in the Royal Marines as a university cadet before deciding on a career in theatrical production. He took considerable flak for taking the rather brave decision not to remain in the services. He is Commodore-in-Chief of the Royal Fleet Auxiliary.

THE DUKE OF CAMBRIDGE

Prince William received his commission as an officer of the British Army at Sandhurst in 2006 and joined the Household Cavalry (the Blues and Royals) as a second lieutenant. He received his Wings from his father at RAF Cranwell (as The Prince of Wales had done from The Duke of Edinburgh more than 40 years earlier) and became a fully operational helicopter pilot with the Royal Air Force's Search and Rescue Force in 2010. He flies Sea King helicopters out of RAF Valley in Wales and is known as Flight-Lieutenant Wales. He also holds the rank of Commodore-in-Chief for Scotland and for submarines.

He is Honorary Air Commandant of Royal Air Force Coningsby and Royal Colonel of the Irish Guards. It is The Duke's first honorary appointment in the army, and His Royal Highness has become the Irish Guards' first Royal Colonel.

PRINCE HENRY OF WALES

Prince Harry, like his brother, attended the Royal Military Academy at Sandhurst and received his commission in 2006, also joining the Blues and Royals. He served for two months in Afghanistan from 2007–8 and has qualified as a helicopter pilot with the Army Air Corps. He is a very highly regarded flier, winning a prize as best co-pilot gunner, and he will be assigned to an Apache Squadron as a fully qualified pilot in the Army Air Corps Attack Helicopter Force.

THE PRINCESS ROYAL

The Princess Royal holds the rank of Rear Admiral and is Chief Commandant for Women in the Royal Navy. She has a special relationship with HMS *Talent* and HMS *Albion*, both of which she launched, and is Commodore-in-Chief, Portsmouth. She is also president of the Women's Section of the Royal British Legion.

THE HOUSEHOLD DIVISION

The Queen is guarded by seven regiments that are collectively known as the Household Division. Two of them are mounted regiments – the Life Guards and the Blues and Royals; and five of them – the Coldstream Guards, the Grenadier Guards, the Scots, the Irish and the Welsh Guards – are foot regiments.

These are the regiments which, as well as being front-line soldiers, fulfil the ceremonial roles in London – guarding The Queen and taking part in processions, royal weddings and such ceremonies as Trooping the Colour and the State Opening of Parliament. They also provide the guards – mounted, or on foot by sentry boxes – outside the royal palaces.

- **The Life Guards**: founded in 1651; they were originally made up of those troops who remained loyal to Charles II after the Civil War.

- **The Blues and Royals**: formed in 1969 from an amalgamation of the Royal Horse Guards whose uniform was blue, and the 1st Royal Dragoons.

The foot regiments can be distinguished from one another by the pattern of their buttons and their collar emblems:

- **The Coldstream Guards** (founded 1650): buttons in pairs and a badge in the form of a garter star.

- **The Grenadier Guards** (founded 1656): single buttons and a collar badge in the shape of a grenade.

- **The Scots Guards** (founded 1686): buttons grouped in threes and a thistle-shaped badge.

- **The Irish Guards** (founded 1900): buttons grouped in fours and a shamrock-shaped badge.

- **The Welsh Guards** (founded 1915): buttons grouped in fives and a badge in the form of a leek.

MILITARY HONOURS

Recommended to Her Majesty The Queen by the Ministry of Defence (advised by commanding officers).

THE VICTORIA CROSS (VC)

Instituted by Queen Victoria in 1856 for acts of extreme bravery 'in the face of the enemy', it is only awarded in exceptional circumstances. While 1,356 Victoria Crosses have been awarded in the medal's history, only 13 VCs have been awarded since the Second World War. The VC may be awarded to servicemen and women of any rank.

The George Cross (GC)

Instituted by King George VI in 1940 for exceptional acts of bravery not 'in the face of the enemy' (for example bomb disposal). The GC may be awarded to servicemen and women and to civilians. Since the medal's inception, 87 GCs have been awarded posthumously and 74 to living recipients.

Distinguished Service Order (DSO)

Recognizes outstanding leadership during active operations and dates back to Queen Victoria's reign in 1886.

George Medal (GM)

Created in 1940 by King George VI at the height of the Blitz, the GM is awarded to civilians for outstanding acts of bravery and to service personnel for bravery not in the face of the enemy.

The Distinguished Service Cross (DSC), the Military Cross (MC) and the Distinguished Flying Cross (DFC)

also recognize acts of bravery.

Mentioned in Despatches

The oldest form of recognition for gallantry during active service operations within the UK armed forces. No medal is awarded, but the citations are published in the *London Gazette*. The Duke of Edinburgh was mentioned in despatches for his actions at the Battle of Matapan in 1941.

THE ELIZABETH CROSS

Instituted by The Queen in 2009, this medal is granted to the next-of-kin of members of the armed forces killed in action on medal-earning operations, or as a result of terrorism. Intended as a mark of national respect, the award is the first to have been created since the George Medal.

THE FIRST GULF WAR

On 2 August 1990 the name of Saddam Hussein became common currency when Iraqi troops, at the behest of their president, invaded oil-rich Kuwait. British hostages (whom he described as his 'guests') were taken in an attempt to avoid conflict with the United Nations while retaining Kuwait. Operation Desert Storm was launched by the United States who amassed 30,000 troops in neighbouring Saudi Arabia. The Iraqis were driven out of Kuwait by a coalition force of 700,000 men from 34 nations in what Saddam Hussein described as "the mother of all battles". Britain sent 25,000 troops, four warships and 60 strike aircraft.

It was assumed by many that the Iraqi troops would be driven back to their capital of Baghdad and their leader removed from power, but that was not the case. Hostilities ended at the Kuwait-Iraq border on 28 February 1991 and their leader lived to fight another day. Departing Iraqi forces set fire to Kuwait's oilfields, and the conflagration took some time to bring under control – the last fire was extinguished in November 1991, nine months after the war had ended.

It would be another 12 years before Saddam Hussein was finally overthrown.

BOSNIA

The break-up of Yugoslavia gave rise to the conflict which took place in Bosnia and Herzegovina between April 1992 and December 1995 when the Bosnian Serb leader Radovan Karadzic declared a new republic (the Republica Srpska) which was supported by the Serbian leader Slobodan Milosevic. The events which followed his declaration gave rise to the worst scenes of ethnic cleansing the world has seen since World War II, with harrowing examples of genocide and the indiscriminate shelling of civilians.

The Bosnian Serb army, under General Ratko Mladic, surrounded Sarajevo and laid siege to the city for nearly four years, during the course of which 10,000 civilians lost their lives. The United Nations set up a so-called safe area in Srebrenica but there, in 1995, forces led by General Mladic massacred 8,000 Muslim boys and men considered to be of an age to fight.

The conflict was finally brought to an end in December 1995 with the signing in Paris of a framework agreement for peace, and the 'Dayton Agreement' itself, signed in Ohio later that month.

The British Army was involved in peace-keeping activities with NATO and the UN and in distributing and protecting convoys carrying humanitarian aid. Milosevic, Karadzic and Mladic were all arrested and charged with war crimes. Milosevic died in his cell in 2006; verdicts are yet to be brought against Karadzic and Mladic.

"The peace and tranquillity of the Norfolk countryside make me realize how fortunate we are and all the more conscious of the trials and sorrows that so many people are suffering both in this country and around the world. My heart goes out to those whose lives have been blighted by war, terrorism, famine, natural disaster or economic hardship. Like many other families, we have lived through some difficult days this year. The prayers, understanding

and sympathy given to us by so many of you, in
good times and bad, have lent us great support and
encouragement. It has touched me deeply that much of
this has come from those of you who have troubles of
your own. As some of you may have heard me
observe, it has, indeed, been a sombre year."

THE QUEEN'S CHRISTMAS MESSAGE, 1992

THE "ANNUS HORRIBILIS"

The Queen celebrated her 40th year on the throne and her
45th wedding anniversary in 1992, a year that was made
even more memorable by a series of unfortunate events that
were summarized by The Queen in a speech at The Guildhall (made all the more poignant by the heavy cold which
gave her a croaky voice): "The past year is not one I shall
look back on with undiluted pleasure. In the words of one
of my more sympathetic correspondents, it has turned out
to be an annus horribilis."

The "sympathetic correspondent" was Sir Edward
Ford, assistant private secretary to The Queen from 1952
until his retirement in 1967, and to her father King George
VI from 1946–52. Sir Edward's invented phrase – thanks
to its razor-like accuracy – has since passed into the history

books. That year saw unfortunate and deeply sad events pile one on top of another:

January   Revelations surrounding The Duchess of York's affair with Texan Steve Wyatt and the fact that they were photographed in Morocco while in the company of the young Princesses Beatrice and Eugenie. (The Duke and Duchess officially separate in March of that year.)

April   Princess Anne and Captain Mark Phillips divorce, having been separated for three years.

June   *Diana – Her True Story* by Andrew Morton reveals information about the breakdown in the marriage of The Prince and Princess of Wales. It is reputed to have the co-operation of The Princess herself and is serialized in the *Sunday Times*.

August   More photos of The Duchess of York and Steve Wyatt appear. Just four days later the *Sun* publishes a transcribed 'hacked' telephone conversation of shared intimacies between Princess Diana and a former boyfriend James Gilbey.

November   The fire at Windsor Castle. Six days later, Prime Minister John Major announces that The Queen and The Prince of Wales have agreed voluntarily to pay income tax on their private incomes – a decision taken in advance of the fire but which is seen by some as a softener to the public in terms of paying for the restoration work. (In reality, the opening of Buckingham Palace to summer visitors would help defray costs.)

December   The prime minister announces the separation of The Prince and Princess of Wales.

THE WINDSOR CASTLE FIRE

On 20 November 1992, the very day of The Queen's 45th wedding anniversary, a fire started in The Queen's Private Chapel at Windsor Castle. Thought to have been ignited by a spotlight setting fire to a curtain, by the time the alarm had been raised, flames had engulfed the northeast corner of the castle. Nine state apartments and around a hundred other rooms were damaged or destroyed, around one-fifth of the Castle area. It took 15 hours and one-and-a-half million gallons of water to put out the blaze. Prince Andrew led the immediate rescue of art works, and all but one of the valuable pictures were saved, as a human chain was formed to ferry the history of a nation to safety.

Images remain of that dreadful night – of the castle silhouetted by the glow of fire; of The Queen in mac, head-scarf and wellies looking on as the fire raged; of countless fire engines and of firemen with hoses endeavouring to quench a blaze that seemed to be intent on destroying the very seat of the British monarchy. One did not have to be a royalist to feel a sense of loss that night, as centuries of British history went up in smoke.

The building and its contents were not insured. The expense was met not by the British public (though the Castle belongs to the nation and is not one of The Queen's private residences) but from the privy purse – the sover-eign's private income.

The restoration was completed six months ahead of schedule on 20 November 1997 at a cost of £37 million, £3 million below budget. Seventy per cent of the necessary revenue was raised from opening Buckingham Palace's State Rooms to visitors in August and September. The remaining 30 per cent of the cost was met from savings in the annual grant-in-aid funding from Parliament for the maintenance and upkeep of the occupied royal palaces.

Prince Philip spearheaded the restoration and took the opportunity to incorporate some of the castle's medieval origins in the new works – opening up the entrance to St George's Hall and creating a new and intimate private chapel with a stained glass window that paid tribute to those involved in saving the Castle from ruin. The fire resulted in the greatest historic building project to have been undertaken in this country in the twentieth century, reviving many traditional crafts.

The opening up of Buckingham Palace during the royal family's summer holiday in Scotland was seen as a good way to help fund the restoration. The summer openings began in 1993 and continued thereafter with the funds being used towards the upkeep of the Royal Collection.

Having drawn on skilled tradesmen to carve masonry and woodwork, to recreate elaborate plaster mouldings, and for gilding, decorating and furnishing, the restoration work continued ceaselessly for five years. To mark the completion, The Queen and The Duke of Edinburgh held a 'thank you' reception in the restored rooms on 14 November 1997 for 1,500 contractors. On 20 November that year they celebrated their golden wedding anniversary with a ball, also held at Windsor Castle. In December, The Queen's Christmas broadcast was made from the Castle's White Drawing Room – produced for the first time by ITV, having previously been the province of the BBC. From now on the honours would alternate. In 2011 Sky Television was responsible for the production of the broadcast.

KEY EVENTS IN THE 1990s

A decade in which the Internet would link up computers all over the world, allowing ordinary people access to all kinds of information and contact with each other – quickly and easily. Mobile phone sizes shrink and become indispensable to every individual – however young! Computer games become hugely popular, especially with the young ...

1990   Mrs Thatcher resigns on 22 November after 11 consecutive years in power. John Major, aged 47, takes over – the youngest prime minister (at that point) in the twentieth century.

1992   Betty Boothroyd is elected the first female speaker of the House of Commons. The BBC makes the film *Elizabeth R* which follows The Queen's life. The press become more and more intrusive on the royal family.

1993   A British female pilot becomes the first woman to fly Concorde.

1994   To mark the 25th anniversary of his investiture, The Prince of Wales authorizes a biography and a TV series about his life. Within it he admits to Jonathan Dimbleby that he had been unfaithful to Diana, but only after the marriage had failed. The Channel Tunnel is opened by The Queen and President Mitterrand.

1997   Dolly the sheep is cloned by scientists at the Roslin
        Institute.

THE PRINCESS OF WALES

From the start Diana was a magnet for the press, growing ever more poised – and more beautiful – as the years passed. She also quickly became very sophisticated in the way she managed her relationship with the media. With looks and a figure to die for, magazines discovered that their circulations would soar with a picture of her on the cover, and her personal style was supremely engaging. She was the first member of the royal family to be photographed hugging a sick child, and she demonstrated a different kind of warmth than the nation was used to from royalty.

Clearly concerned and compassionate towards those in need, she visited AIDS wards, sat with the sick and held their hands, cuddled babies, laughed with people and shared their tears without apparent embarrassment. It was a rare gift, and to be in her presence was to feel a kind of magnetism. Most men, on the receiving end of one of her glances – the blue eyes flashing from under the lowered eyelids – would find themselves lost for words.

Dressmakers loved her, and as her confidence became more assured, so, too, did her ability to act as an ambassador for Britain's fashion houses. Within just a few years she became the most photographed and most admired woman in the world.

After a gloriously happy start to the marriage and the birth of two sons adored by both their parents, it all went wrong. Eventually, on 9 December 1992, it was announced that Charles and Diana were formally to separate.

But further unhappy revelations continued and The Queen, conscious of the damage that could be done to all parties – and to the monarchy as a whole – by the ongoing, very public marriage breakdown, wrote to both Charles and Diana asking them to agree to a divorce. They did so on 28 August 1996. Diana relinquished the title 'Her Royal Highness', becoming simply, Lady Diana, Princess of Wales.

Subsequently Diana threw herself into charity work. She had told her television interviewer, Martin Bashir, that she wanted to be "queen of people's hearts". It was a tragically short-lived role.

"We all felt the shock and sorrow of Diana's death. Thousands upon thousands of you expressed your grief most poignantly in the wonderful flowers and messages left

*The early days of Princess Diana's marriage to Prince Charles
were picture-perfect, but tragedy was to strike.*

in tribute to her. That was a great comfort to all those close to her, while people all around the world joined us here in Britain for that service in Westminster Abbey."

THE QUEEN'S CHRISTMAS MESSAGE, 1997

THE DEATH OF DIANA

Diana's death, at the age of 36, shook the world. It affected our perception of the monarchy and, for a time, it seemed that nothing would ever be the same again. In some ways this proved to be the case.

After her divorce, Diana had a number of relationships. That with Dodi Al Fayed, the son of the owner of Harrods and the Paris Ritz began in 1996. In July 1997 Diana and her sons spent a holiday in the South of France at the home of Mohammed Al Fayed. The boys then went to Balmoral to be with their father while Diana continued her holiday with Dodi, first on Sardinia and then on Al Fayed's yacht in the Mediterranean. Speculation was rife as to the seriousness of their relationship and the likelihood of Diana marrying an Egyptian muslim who would then become stepfather to two heirs to the British throne. It was rumoured that he had bought a ring. The media, who had adored The Princess, was beginning to take a more jaundiced view of her behaviour.

At the end of the holiday the couple took a trip to Paris where, on 30 August, they had supper at the Ritz. During the drive from the hotel to Dodi's apartment, their car – which was being pursued at high speed by several members of the paparazzi – crashed into a pillar of the tunnel under the Place de l'Alma, killing Dodi and the driver Henri Paul instantly and leaving Diana mortally injured. For two hours, surgeons fought to save her life in the Pitié-Salpêtrière hospital, but she was pronounced dead at 3 a.m. (British Summer Time) the following morning. It was a Sunday. The only survivor was Diana's bodyguard Trevor Rees-Jones who had no memory of the accident.

From the moment the news became known, floral tributes began to pile up outside the gates of Buckingham Palace and Diana's London home at Kensington Palace; books of condolence were opened – one after another as they rapidly filled up. The surge of emotion was unprecedented. Day after day the sea of floral tributes increased and the public became uneasy at the thought of the royal family apparently cocooned in their Scottish castle at Balmoral while the nation mourned. No flag flew at half mast from Buckingham Palace. Had the royal family no sympathy?

The reality was that The Queen and The Prince of Wales were anxious to shield and comfort the two young Princes – who had just lost their mother – away from the prying eyes of the world while their father went to Paris to bring home the body of The Princess. "We must get them away from the television," she said; and at Balmoral the preferred alternative of fresh air and exercise was readily available. Peter Phillips, The Princess Royal's son, took the boys out every day on all-terrain vehicles, and most evenings the family went off in the Land Rover towing their picnic trailer to a shooting lodge on the estate. In Scotland they would be safe and secure, surrounded by their family at a time when the grief of the two young Princes – aged 15 and 12 – must have been profound. The flag above Buckingham Palace was not flown at half-mast simply because the Royal Standard – the only flag ever flown there – is *never* flown at half mast. It is flown to signify The Queen's presence and is either up or down.

The royal family had planned to stay together in Scotland until the day before the funeral, but five days after Diana's death The Queen and The Duke of Edinburgh returned to London and were filmed viewing the floral tributes laid outside the gates of Buckingham Palace. There were worries that the crowds might be hostile; in the event they were not – the family was warmly welcomed.

That night The Queen broadcast a message to the nation from Buckingham Palace in which she said: "What I say to you now as your Queen, as a grandmother, I say from my heart ... Diana was an exceptional and gifted human being. I admired and respected her ..." Later in the same broadcast she added: "Lessons have been learned."

Indeed they had – but by the nation, as well as by the monarchy. Perhaps it finally dawned on us that although we treat the royal family as being different from us (as indeed they are, and as they must appear in order to sustain Bagehot's 'magic'), they are still human beings and members of a family who feel grief in exactly the same way as we do. To deny them that right would be unreasonable, unrealistic and cruel. It is also unrealistic to expect them to be free of human frailty.

But the event did demonstrate the huge impact that Diana had had on not only the people of Britain but also on those around the world. She would never be forgotten.

Symbolically, from that day on, when the sovereign is not in residence at Buckingham Palace, the Union Flag is flown. It was flown at half mast over the palace to mark Diana's death in the face of public pressure. A small but significant part of royal protocol was changed.

The Prince of Wales overruled protocol experts who suggested that as Diana was no longer a member of the royal family her funeral should be a private affair organized by the Spencer family. The Prince insisted that the late mother of a future king should be accorded a ceremonial funeral (state funerals are reserved, with very few exceptions – Winston Churchill being one – for monarchs). In according Diana the honour of a national ceremonial funeral, The Prince correctly picked up the mood of the country.

The funeral was arranged in less than a week. The night before, Kensington Gardens was filled with crowds of mourners who maintained an all-night vigil, bringing yet more flowers and lighted candles.

At 9.08 a.m. on 6 September a horse-drawn gun carriage bearing Diana's coffin draped in her personal standard left Kensington Palace. Twelve soldiers from the Welsh Guards – the Princess of Wales's royal regiment – flanked the coffin. On top of The Princess's standard were three white floral tributes. One was from The Princess's brother; the other two were from her sons. The word 'Mummy' could be glimpsed in the centre of a circlet of white rosebuds; it was from Prince Harry. A bell in the tower of Westminster Abbey tolled every minute as the cortege travelled through streets thickly lined with mourners. The occasional heart-rending cry rang out; but most people were silent and all that could be heard on that sunny morning was the clattering of hooves and the jingling of harnesses.

As the gun carriage passed Buckingham Palace The Queen, standing outside the gates, bowed her head. At St James's Palace, The Prince of Wales, Princes William and Harry, The Duke of Edinburgh and Earl Spencer, Diana's brother, fell in behind the gun carriage and walked behind it all the way to Westminster Abbey, where the funeral service was conducted by the Archbishop of Canterbury in front of a congregation of 1,900 people – many of them drawn from the world of fashion and entertainment (Diana's Christmas card list helped with the selection of those invited).

Prime Minster Tony Blair read – a touch theatrically – from St Paul's 1st Letter to the Corinthians. Elton John sang 'Candle in the Wind', changing the words to 'Goodbye England's Rose', which went on to sell over 30 million copies; and Earl Spencer used the occasion to praise his sister and take something of a swipe at the royal family. His speech was greeted with applause outside the abbey, which spread to those inside. It was an uncomfortable moment, although it captured the mood of some of the nation. With hindsight it was not only harsh but ill judged and profoundly unfair. The Prince of Wales could not have given Princes William and Harry a happier or more secure upbringing and insisted on shielding them from the spotlight of the media for as long as he could.

After the ceremony the coffin was taken by car to Northamptonshire – with onlookers throwing flowers from motorway bridges as it passed. On the Spencer estate, Althorp, Diana's body was interred on an island in a lake. The Prince of Wales and his two sons were there, along with Diana's mother and her immediate family.

The television coverage of Diana's funeral attracted 31 million viewers in the UK and two and a half billion worldwide.

Inevitably, ridiculous conspiracy theories began to spring up surrounding her death. The simple reality was that it was an accident caused by a driver who had drunk too much and was going too fast to escape from the paparazzi.

There were those who thought that the death of Diana – so popular and so universally loved, despite the flaws in her personality – would be the beginning of the end for the monarchy. It transpired that such an assumption underestimated the deeper feelings of the nation; feelings that had been developed over more than 50 years and which would be strong enough to see The Queen and the whole royal family through probably the most difficult time in her reign.

"But Prince Philip and I also knew the joy of our golden wedding. We were glad to be able to share this at Buckingham Palace with many other couples, who are celebrating their 50th anniversary this year."

THE QUEEN'S CHRISTMAS MESSAGE, 1997

THE QUEEN'S GOLDEN WEDDING ANNIVERSARY

A service of thanksgiving at Westminster Abbey, meeting the crowds outside, and then drinks with Prime Minister Tony

Blair at 10 Downing Street before a lunchtime banquet at the Mansion House marked The Queen and The Duke's golden wedding anniversary on 20 November 1997. The Queen's speech on that day not only reminded the nation of what she and The Duke had lived through, but also reflected her well-developed sense of humour:

When Prince Philip and I were married on this day 50 years ago, Britain had just endured six years of war, emerging battered but victorious. Prince Philip had served in the Royal Navy in the Far East, while I was grappling, in the ATS, with the complexities of the combustion engine and learning to drive an ambulance with care ...

"What a remarkable 50 years they have been: for the world, for the Commonwealth and for Britain. Think what we would have missed if we had never heard The Beatles or seen Margot Fonteyn dance; never have watched television, used a mobile telephone or surfed the Net (or, to be honest, listened to other people talking about surfing the Net).

"We would never have heard someone speak from the Moon; never have watched England win the World Cup or Red Rum three Grand Nationals. We would never have heard that Everest had been scaled, DNA unravelled, the Channel Tunnel built, hip replacements become commonplace. Above all, speaking personally, we

would never have known the joys of having children and grandchildren.

"As you say Prime Minister, since I came to the throne in 1952, ten prime ministers have served the British people and have come to see me each week at Buckingham Palace. The first, Winston Churchill, had charged with the cavalry at Omdurman. You, Prime Minister, were born in the year of my coronation.

It was a point nicely made. The Queen's experience of life is second to none.

A set of commemorative stamps was issued on 13 November, and the Royal Mint struck a five-pound coin to celebrate the occasion.

The conclusion of The Queen's speech was particularly touching:

All too often, I fear, Prince Philip has had to listen to me speaking. Frequently we have discussed my intended speech beforehand and, as you will imagine, his views have been expressed in a forthright manner.

"He is someone who doesn't take easily to compliments but he has, quite simply, been my strength and stay all these years, and I, and his whole family, and this and many other countries, owe him a debt greater than he would ever claim, or we shall ever know.

PRINCE EDWARD MARRIES SOPHIE RHYS-JONES

Two hundred million people worldwide were estimated to have watched the marriage of The Queen's third son to PR executive Sophie Rhys-Jones in St George's Chapel, Windsor, and 15,000 lined the 3-mile route of the procession through the town. The marriage was conducted by the Bishop of Norwich, and the couple deliberately chose to have a low-key ceremony with which the public could become more involved, rather than an elaborate state affair at Westminster Abbey.

The Queen announced that the couple would be known as The Earl and Countess of Wessex, and it was also announced that when the title of Duke of Edinburgh reverted to the Crown (after Prince Philip's death), it would be assumed by Prince Edward.

The couple endeavoured to continue their working lives to some extent – The Prince having left Andrew Lloyd-Webber's Really Useful Group to set up his own company, Ardent Productions. But by 2002 this situation was found to have become unworkable (there was an incident, yet again involving a tabloid newspaper, where The Countess was accused of using her position to further her business). Thereafter the couple took on more royal duties, The Earl taking over much of Prince Philip's work with The Duke of Edinburgh's Award Scheme. The couple now undertake around 550 engagements a year, and The Countess is particularly involved in charities relating to children and disabilities.

The Countess is deservedly popular, and the couple now have two children: Lady Louise Alice Elizabeth Mary, born 8 November 2003, and James Alexander Philip Theo, Viscount Severn (the child takes one of his father's subsidiary titles), born 17 December 2007. With The Queen's agreement the Wessex children have not taken the title 'Prince' and 'Princess', but take courtesy titles as the son and daughter of an earl.

ROYAL WEDDINGS

Arranged by the head of Her Majesty's working household, the Lord Chamberlain, royal weddings are generally planned only six months in advance. The Lord Chamberlain's office, under the executive management of the Comptroller of the Household, will co-ordinate everything from the clergy to the state coaches. The Glass Coach is normally used for royal weddings, though it was replaced by a state landau at the wedding of Prince William and Catherine Middleton. Like other royal coaches and carriages, it is housed in the Royal Mews behind Buckingham Palace.

Before the First World War, royal weddings were usually private affairs that took place in the Chapel Royal at St James's Palace, but the tradition changed in 1923 with the marriage of King George VI and Lady Elizabeth Bowes-Lyon at Westminster Abbey. Most royal weddings since that date have taken place at the abbey, the notable exception being that of The Prince of Wales and Lady Diana Spencer which was held at St Paul's Cathedral.

"This December we are looking back not just on one year, but on a hundred years and a thousand years. History is measured in centuries. More than ever we are aware of being a tiny part of the infinite sweep of time when we move from one century and one millennium to another.

But I do not think we should be over-anxious. We can make sense of the future if we understand the lessons of the past. Winston Churchill, my first prime minister, said that 'the further backward you look, the further forward you can see'."

THE QUEEN'S CHRISTMAS MESSAGE, 1999

THE NEW
MILLENNIUM

"The future is not only about new gadgets, modern technology or the latest fashion, important as these may be. At the centre of our lives – today and tomorrow – must be the message of caring for others, the message at the heart of Christianity and of all the great religions.

"This message – love thy neighbour as thyself – may be for Christians 2,000 years old. But it is as relevant today as it ever was. I believe it gives us the guidance and the reassurance we need as we step over the threshold into the twenty-first century."

THE QUEEN'S CHRISTMAS MESSAGE, 1999

The new millennium was to bring The Queen joy and sadness in equal measure: joy on the occasion of Queen Elizabeth The Queen Mother's 100th birthday, to be followed by the sadness of her death and that of The Queen's sister, Princess Margaret, less than two years later. But the same year also marked The Queen's Golden Jubilee and a chance for the country to celebrate half a century of Queen Elizabeth II's reign as well as the passing of another thousand years.

THE LANDMARKS

There are many images etched into the memories of those who witnessed the arrival of the new millennium, not least that of the massive ferris wheel on London's South Bank that became known as the London Eye. Safety issues delayed its opening, so it was not operational on 31 December 1999, but it has been delighting Londoners and visitors ever since, its slow-moving gondolas offering a fine view right across the capital.

FROM 2000 TO 2011

Prime ministers	Tony Blair (1997–2007); Gordon Brown (2007–10); David Cameron (2010–)
Price of a pint of milk	34p (2000); 45p (2009); 49p (2011)
Price of a loaf of bread	70p (2000); £1.26 (2009); £1.10 (2011)
Price of a dozen eggs	£1.68 (2000); £2.66 (2009)
Price of petrol	396.3p per gallon; 79.9p per litre (2005); 408.7p per gallon, 88p per litre (2009); 630p per gallon, 140p per litre! (2011)
Average weekly wage	£550
Average house price	£130,000 (2000); £228,000 (2010)
On TV	Big Brother; The X-Factor; Britain's Got Talent; I'm a Celebrity Get Me Out of Here; Spooks; Bleak House; Strictly Come Dancing; Lark Rise to Candleford; The Weakest Link; Downton Abbey; Call the Midwife

"Christmas is the traditional, if not the actual, birthday
of a man who was destined to change the course of our
history. And today we are celebrating the fact that
Jesus Christ was born 2,000 years ago; this is
the true millennium anniversary.

"Even in our very material age the impact of Christ's life is
all around us. If you want to see an expression of Christian
faith you have only to look at our awe-inspiring cathedrals
and abbeys, listen to their music, or look at their stained
glass windows, their books and their pictures.

"But the true measure of Christ's influence is not
only in the lives of the saints but also in the good works
quietly done by millions of men and women day
in and day out throughout the centuries."

THE QUEEN'S CHRISTMAS MESSAGE, 2000

THE QUEEN'S ROLE AS DEFENDER OF THE FAITH

While the Archbishop of Canterbury is Primate of All
England (and head of the worldwide Anglican church) and

therefore head of the Church of England, The Queen has the title 'Defender of the Faith and Supreme Governor of the Church of England'. In her coronation oath she promised to maintain the church, and her role is that of providing moral and spiritual leadership.

The Queen invests bishops, attends festivals, memorials, thanksgivings and other church events, though she only attends the funerals and memorial services of members of her close family, sending a representative on other occasions (a state of affairs which is understandable given the wide circle of those who come into contact with her).

HOW THE CHURCH OF ENGLAND CAME ABOUT

From the time of St Augustine, in the fourth century, right up until the sixteenth century, Archbishops of Canterbury had been Catholic. In 1528 Cardinal Wolsey (Cardinal and Lord Chancellor of England) failed to persuade the Pope to grant King Henry VIII a divorce from his first wife Catherine of Aragon and fell from favour. It was Thomas Cromwell, Chief Minister to The King, who finally arranged the split from Rome so that Henry could obtain a divorce, marry Anne Boleyn and declare himself head of the Church in England. The Dissolution of the Monasteries followed in

1535 and Henry established himself as God's representative on earth: Head of the Church of England as well as Head of State – a position occupied by all monarchs since.

ARCHBISHOPS OF CANTERBURY DURING THE REIGN OF ELIZABETH II

Geoffrey Fisher 1945–61

Michael Ramsay 1961–74

Donald Coggan 1974–80

Robert Runcie 1980–91

George Carey 1991–2002

Rowan Williams 2003–2012

Justin Welby 2013–

RELIGION IN OUR LIVES

During the 60 years of The Queen's reign, it would seem that religion has gradually played a smaller role in people's lives – church attendances are down on those years immediately after the war. Few children now kneel by their beds to say their prayers as they did in the 1950s. Few schools hold a daily 'assembly' when hymns are sung and prayers said. Even in Church of England schools, such events are often, at best, held on a weekly basis.

THE QUEEN MOTHER REACHES 100

From the time of the death of King George VI, Queen Elizabeth The Queen Mother, as she became known, forged her own role within the royal family. While The Queen was at its head, Queen Elizabeth (as she was always known within the royal household) became, in effect, the nation's royal granny. Always outgoing, always recognizable at a distance on account of her love of bright pastel coats and wide-brimmed and often feather-adorned hats, she could light up a room simply by walking into it, or raise spirits with her characteristic wave – palm inwards, describing a circular movement. The older she got, the more the nation loved 'The Queen Mum'.

Encouraged by her friend Lord Mildmay, steeplechasing became a passion and her colours – blue with buff stripes – were a regular feature of National Hunt meetings. She was a successful owner, too – over her racing lifetime her horses won around 500 races. Special Cargo won the 1984 Whitbread Gold Cup but Devon Loch, ridden by Dick Francis (later to become a favourite thriller writer of The Queen

Mother) made headlines by 'belly flopping' a short distance before the winning post when on course to win the 1956 Grand National. Sanguine as ever, The Queen Mother said, "That's racing," and endeavoured to avoid speaking of the incident again.

In the last 20 years of her life, as the media became more generally critical, some members of the press would try to take ill-conceived swipes at The Queen Mother, sometimes for her lifestyle or for her 'out of touch' views. They could not have misread the mood of the nation more. The Queen Mother's decades of service to the country, through its

The ever-popular 'Queen Mum' celebrated her
100th birthday with a service at St Paul's.

darkest and worst days, seemed to put her above reproach. The nation did not just respect her, they loved her.

The Queen Mother's 100th birthday was marked with a service of thanksgiving at St Paul's Cathedral. As she left she stopped to speak to other centenarians who had been invited. "Do you know," she said afterwards (her sense of mischief to the fore), "they were all in wheelchairs."

THE ROLE OF CONSTITUTIONAL MONARCH

Constitutional Monarchy is a form of government in which the sovereign acts as Head of State but does not 'rule' the country. The elected government makes laws, passes Acts of Parliament and runs the country, but the monarch fulfils important formal and ceremonial roles within this system.

HEAD OF STATE

It is part of the monarch's role formally to appoint the prime minister – the politician at the head of the party which commands a majority in the House of Commons. After journeying to the palace, the candidate will be invited to form a government, and must also ask The Queen's permission to call a general election.

HEAD OF NATION

Centuries of continuity, tradition and devotion to a country are, in themselves, of enormous significance and no little comfort to a nation which must undergo a general election and a potential change of political leader every five years. The Queen's history and ancestry is *our* history and ancestry and she provides a stability that no government ever can.

We know that come rain or shine, come Labour, Conservative or Liberal Democrat, The Queen – the sovereign – will still be there. In our ever-changing world the monarchy is the one constant.

ON-SCREEN ADVANCES

The 'noughties', as they became amusingly called, saw DVDs replacing video tapes as the preferred means of watching films at home. They also saw the rise of 'online' communication via the internet, of 'broadband', which made such access even more rapid, and of 'search engines' like Google, which could locate information on a mind-bogglingly wide range of topics through such websites as 'Wikipedia', which has brought encyclopaedic information within the grasp of anyone who is connected to the worldwide web.

Instead of making a phone call, friends could stay in touch on 'Facebook' and 'Twitter' and in 2007 Apple produced their first iPhone, followed by the iPad in 2010. These mobile communication devices, along with a range of thousands of applications ('apps'), provide everything from amusing games to news and weather forecasts as well as information on places to eat and films to see. Online shopping took off and websites such as Amazon offered the delivery of books and all manner of goods within 24 hours. The e-book (in particular Amazon's Kindle) took off in 2010, bringing fears that paper books would soon become a thing of the past. Only time will tell.

AFGHANISTAN

In 2001 the words 'Nine-eleven' (the Americanization of the date) were to become a part of the English vocabulary. On 11 September 2001, two hijacked commercial airliners were flown into the twin towers of the World Trade Center in New York, destroying them. Similar attacks were made at the same time in Washington DC and Pennsylvania, though the action of passengers prevented a direct hit on the Pentagon. In total 2,752 civilians lost their lives.

The American president, George W. Bush, declared war on what he called "the axis of evil" – identifying the perpetrators as a terrorist organization comprising Al Qaeda (a militant Islamic group founded by Osama bin Laden) and the group that sheltered it – the equally militant Taliban. The war in Afghanistan began on 7 October 2001 when US armed forces launched Operation Enduring Freedom. Troops from many different countries were involved, but US and British armed forces sent the lion's share. The aim was to dismantle Al Qaeda and to end its use of Afghanistan as a base for terrorist operations, as well as removing the Taliban from power and restoring Afghanistan to a democratic state.

In just a few weeks the Taliban was ousted from power and many of its leaders fled to neighbouring Pakistan. An interim government was created and an International Security Assistance Force under the aegis of the UN and subsequently NATO was put in position as a peacekeeping force, comprising troops from the 42 NATO countries.

On 2 May 2011, Osama bin Laden was caught and shot dead at his house near a military compound in Pakistan. Two other Al Qaeda leaders were killed shortly afterwards, and over the next few years both the US and British governments plan a gradual withdrawal of troops in the hope that some kind of stability can be brought to a country that has already engaged British troops in three Anglo–Afghan wars: first in 1839–42, secondly in 1878–80, thirdly in 1919 and now since 2001.

ROYAL WOOTTON BASSETT

A small market town close to RAF Lyneham in Wiltshire, Wootton Bassett made a name for itself during the time of the conflicts in Afghanistan and Iraq by virtue of the respect it showed on the repatriation of those killed in wars overseas. Those servicemen and women who had lost their lives would be flown home into RAF Lyneham, just four miles from the town, in a Hercules aircraft. At first the friends and relatives of the fallen would stand in the streets of Wootton Bassett and local representatives of The Royal British Legion and others would join them as a mark of respect. Soon word spread, and people from further afield

The residents of Royal Wootton Bassett acknowledged the sacrifices made by servicemen and women overseas.

would come to join the local community in paying tribute to the fallen. The bell of the local church would be tolled as the procession made its way slowly and silently through the town, bystanders quietly lining the main street as each funeral cortege passed. In 2009 Prince William presented the town with an award in recognition of its role, and The Prince of Wales and The Duchess of Cornwall laid a wreath on the local war memorial in 2010.

In recognition of its role during repatriations, the town was granted royal patronage by The Queen in March 2011 and became Royal Wootton Bassett. Since the closure of RAF Lyneham in September 2011 the repatriations now take place at RAF Brize Norton in Oxfordshire.

THE CONTINUITY OF THE MONARCHY

The role of monarch is inherited, unlike those of president and prime minister which are determined by election. At the moment the role of sovereign passes on the death of one king or queen to the next in a line of succession which favours the eldest male child in preference to all others, but there are signs now that this will change in the not-too-distant future. The firstborn of The Duke and Duchess of Cambridge is likely to inherit the throne whether he or she is a male or female.

"As I look back over these past 12 months, I know that it has been about as full a year as I can remember ...

"Many of you will know only too well, from your own experience, the grief that follows the death of a much loved mother or sister. Mine were very much a part of my life and always gave me their support and encouragement.

"But my own sadness was tempered by the generous tributes that so many of you paid to the service they gave to this country and the wider Commonwealth.

"At such a difficult time this gave me great comfort and inspiration as I faced up both to my own personal loss and to the busy Jubilee summer ahead ..."

THE QUEEN'S CHRISTMAS MESSAGE, 2002

THE DEATHS OF PRINCESS MARGARET AND THE QUEEN MOTHER

"When sorrows come, they come not single spies, but in battalions," says Claudius in Shakespeare's *Hamlet*. In 2002, for The Queen, they may not have come in battalions, but certainly there were two great sorrows. Princess Margaret, younger than The Queen by four years, died on 9 February 2002 at the age of 71. A heavy smoker, until the age of 60 when she gave up, Princess Margaret had undergone a lung operation in 1985 and suffered several debilitating strokes during the last few years of her life. After one final stroke she died in King Edward VII Hospital in London and a private funeral was held in St George's Chapel, Windsor, after which the Princess was cremated (at her own request). Her ashes would later be interred in the chapel beside the remains of her mother and father.

In the Princess's final years she seemed, to onlookers, a forlorn figure. She had been badly scalded by a hot bath at her holiday home on the island of Mustique in 1999, which had impaired her mobility and resulted in her last public appearances being made in a wheelchair and wearing dark glasses. It was a sad end to a life that had once seemed so glittering and carefree.

The Queen Mother's last few years had seen her becoming increasingly frail – she fell and broke her pelvis in December 2001 at the age of 101, but still insisted on standing for the national anthem at the memorial service for her late husband King George VI on 6 February 2002. Just three days later her younger daughter died and to The Queen's dismay Queen Elizabeth insisted on travelling from Sandringham to Windsor for the funeral.

Queen Elizabeth's eventful life finally drew to a close on 30 March 2002 when she died in her sleep at Royal Lodge, Windsor, with The Queen at her side. It was Easter weekend. Aged 101, The Queen Mother was, at the time, the longest-lived member of the royal family in British history (an honour that passed to her sister-in-law Princess Alice, Duchess of Gloucester, who died on 29 October 2004 aged 102).

The Queen Mother's body was taken from Royal Lodge on 5 April to lie in state in Westminster Hall. Upon the coffin lay camellias from her own garden. Over three days, 200,000 people filed past the catafalque (a public response not expected by the government nor the media of the day), guarded at one point by her four grandsons – the vigil of the Princes.

On the day of the state funeral, 9 April, more than a million people stood outside Westminster Abbey and lined the route from London to Windsor where Queen Elizabeth was laid to rest beside her late husband in St George's Chapel, the ashes of their younger daughter alongside them. At The Queen Mother's request, the wreath that had lain on her coffin was placed upon the Tomb of the Unknown Soldier in Westminster Abbey, as was her bouquet on the day of her wedding.

The day of the funeral was fine and clear. I stood with my wife halfway down The Mall as the hearse bearing The

Queen Mother's body passed quite slowly, closely followed by a car carrying The Prince of Wales who would accompany the body on its journey to Windsor. There was a longer gap before The Queen's car passed, at which point the crowds on either side of The Mall broke into gentle, heartfelt and sympathetic applause. The most senior member of the royal family had passed away and, at that moment, or so it seemed, the mantle had passed to her daughter.

THE GOLDEN JUBILEE

Only three British monarchs have managed to celebrate 50 years on the throne – King George III was the first, in 1809; Queen Victoria celebrated hers in 1887; and Queen Elizabeth II had reigned for 50 years in 2002.

The celebrations began on 1 May when The Queen toured the UK and visited parts of the Commonwealth – Jamaica, Australia, New Zealand and Canada – travelling a total of 40,000 miles by air.

There were street parties all over the world – even British scientists in Antarctica celebrated with an outdoor feast, a game of cricket and perfectly chilled champagne (in a temperature of minus 20 degrees).

The 'Party at the Palace' was a two-day extravaganza over the extended Jubilee weekend of 1–4 June. It involved two televised concerts from the gardens of Buckingham Palace – one pop, one classical – the pop concert opening with 'Queen' guitarist Brian May playing an unforgettable rock version of the national anthem from the roof of the palace. The show was watched by The Queen from a tented grandstand and by a crowd of 12,000, while a further 200 million worldwide watched the televised version. The recorded version sold 100,000 copies on CD in the first week of its release which resulted in The Queen being awarded a Gold Disc by the record industry!

On 4 June a Jubilee parade took place on The Mall, where decorated floats bearing all kinds of people from all walks of life celebrated The Queen's long reign. One particular float carried 'British icons' – luminaries such as Sir Cliff Richard, Sir Cameron Mackintosh and ... er ... me! It was a day to be remembered for ever: the cheering crowds, the hugely warm atmosphere, and The Queen and The Duke of Edinburgh sitting at the foot of the Queen Victoria Memorial in front of Buckingham Palace and acknowledging the floats as they passed. I found myself standing next to a small blonde lady as we waved at The Queen. She noticed us and turned to The Duke. I could lip-read her words quite clearly. "Look!" she said. "It's Barbara Windsor."

"I felt the Golden Jubilee was more than just an anniversary. The celebrations were joyous occasions, but they also seemed to evoke something more lasting and profound – a sense of belonging and pride in country, town or community; a sense of sharing a common heritage enriched by the cultural, ethnic and religious diversity of our twenty-first-century society."

THE QUEEN'S CHRISTMAS MESSAGE, 2002

THE SECOND GULF WAR

Sanctions were maintained against Iraq by US president Bill Clinton after the first Gulf War, and Saddam Hussein was required to relinquish all 'weapons of mass destruction' (WMD). After 11 September 2001 ('Nine-eleven') the new US president, George W. Bush, believed that the Iraqi regime was sheltering Al-Qaeda. Unnamed intelligence sources suggested that Saddam had the capability of launching WMD within 45 minutes, which were capable of reaching targets in the west. This 'intelligence' led to the US sending 148,000 troops and Prime Minister Tony Blair 45,000, augmented by forces from Poland and Australia.

The initial invasion took place between 19 March and 9 April 2003 and 36 other countries became involved subsequently. The attack began with an air strike on the presidential palace in Baghdad, followed by an incursion into Basra province, all with the aim of disarming the WMD, removing the threat to world peace, and ending Saddam Hussein's reign of terror.

On 1 May 2003 the invasion was complete and the military occupation began, but not before many lives had been lost.

Saddam Hussein was finally captured in 2003 and after two separate trials was hanged on 30 December 2006.

Thorough inspections and searches took place to locate the alleged weaponry, but in 2005 the US Central Intelligence Agency (CIA) released a report saying that no WMD had been found in Iraq. The lack of weapons produced a backlash against the government in the UK, deploring the loss of life of British troops, seemingly to no avail.

The troops were gradually withdrawn and in a surprise visit to the troops in Baghdad in December 2008, Prime Minister Gordon Brown announced that British troops would leave Iraq in 2009. On 30 April 2009 the British military officially handed over its airbase near Basra to the US, with only a small number of troops remaining after that date to train Iraqi security forces.

THE PRINCE OF WALES MARRIES CAMILLA PARKER BOWLES

On 9 April 2005 (a day later than planned, due to The Prince having to attend the funeral of Pope John Paul II) The Prince of Wales married Camilla Parker Bowles in a civil ceremony at Windsor Guildhall, followed by a service of blessing in St George's Chapel. The witnesses to the marriage were Prince William and Tom Parker Bowles. The Queen and The Duke of Edinburgh led the entire royal family and hundreds of friends and members of The Prince of Wales's Household at the service of blessing. It had been almost nine years since The Prince's divorce and nearly eight years since the death of Diana.

Camilla Shand and The Prince of Wales had first met in 1970, but his naval career, which meant that he was away for long periods of time, meant that their relationship was interrupted.

Camilla Rosemary Shand was born at King's College Hospital, London, on 17 July 1947 and raised in East Sussex by her parents Major Bruce Shand (1917–2006) and the Honourable Rosalind (née Cubitt; 1921–1994). She had a happy home life with her sister, Annabel, to whom she remains particularly close, and her brother, Mark, and was exceptionally fond of her father. The piece of information that many enjoy retelling is that Camilla's maternal great-grandmother, Alice Keppel, had been the mistress of King Edward VII.

At the reception in Windsor Castle The Queen made a generous and affectionate speech expressing her pride in her son, and in the seven years that have followed The Prince of Wales and The Duchess of Cornwall (an alternative title chosen to avoid confusion and comparison with Diana) have endeared themselves more and more to the British public by virtue of their hard work, good nature and tireless support for charitable causes.

"I am reminded of a lady of about my age who was asked by an earnest, little granddaughter the other day, 'Granny, can you remember the Stone Age?' Whilst that may be going a bit far, the older generation are able to give a sense of context as well as the wisdom of experience which can be invaluable."

THE QUEEN'S CHRISTMAS MESSAGE, 2006

THE QUEEN'S 80TH BIRTHDAY

Around 20,000 birthday cards and 17,000 emails were received by The Queen on her 80th birthday, which she celebrated on 21 April 2006 at Windsor Castle. At 8.30 a.m. a giant Royal Standard was raised above the Round Tower – the highest point on the Castle – and at 10.30 a.m. a 21-gun salute was fired on the Long Walk in Windsor Great Park.

It was a happy day, and one enjoyed by the thousands who went to the town to see The Queen and The Duke 'go walkabout' for three-quarters of an hour at lunchtime in the town's High Street – many folk turning up early in the morning with folding chairs to claim a good spot. As The Queen walked through the Castle gates, the band of the Irish Guards played 'Happy Birthday'.

On television that night, The Prince of Wales broadcast a tribute to The Queen in which he recalled his own memories of her reign:

> *... I have vivid memories of the coronation; of my mother coming to say goodnight to my sister and me while wearing the crown so that she could get used to its weight on her head before the coronation ceremony; of thousands of people gathered in The Mall outside*

Buckingham Palace chanting 'We want The Queen' and keeping me awake at night; of my parents being away for long overseas tours during the 1950s and of determined attempts to speak to them on the telephone in far-distant lands when all you could hear was the faintest of voices in a veritable storm of crackling and static interference.

"There is no doubt that the world in which my mother grew up and, indeed, the world in which she first became Queen, has changed beyond all recognition. But during those years she has shown the most remarkable steadfastness and fortitude, always remaining a figure of reassuring calm and dependability – an example to so many of service, duty and devotion in a world of sometimes bewildering change and disorientation.

"For very nearly 60 of those 80 years she has been my darling Mama and my sentiments today are those of a proud and loving son who hopes that you will join me in wishing The Queen the happiest of happy birthdays, together with the fervent prayer that there will be countless memorable returns of the day ...

"Over 400 years ago, King James the Sixth of Scotland inherited the throne of England at a time when the Christian Church was deeply divided. Here at Hampton Court in 1604, he convened a conference of churchmen of all shades of opinion to discuss the future of Christianity in this country. The King agreed to commission a new translation of the Bible that was acceptable to all parties. This was to become the King James, or Authorized, Bible, which next year will be exactly four centuries old.

"Acknowledged as a masterpiece of English prose and the most vivid translation of the scriptures, the glorious language of this Bible has survived the turbulence of history and given many of us the most widely recognized and beautiful descriptions of the birth of Jesus Christ, which we celebrate today.

"The King James Bible was a major cooperative endeavour that required the efforts of dozens of the day's leading scholars. The whole enterprise was guided by an interest in reaching agreement for the wider benefit of the Christian Church, and to bring harmony to the Kingdoms of England and Scotland."

THE QUEEN'S CHRISTMAS MESSAGE, 2010

THE WEDDING OF PRINCE WILLIAM AND CATHERINE MIDDLETON

It was a long-awaited wedding; the couple had an on/off but mainly 'on' relationship for eight years, and finally tied the knot on 29 April 2011. As Prince Philip put it: "They've been practising long enough!" The day itself was declared a public holiday and the service took place in a Westminster Abbey decorated with trees as well as abundant floral decorations – the trees later removed and planted in The Prince of Wales's garden at Highgrove.

Catherine Elizabeth Middleton was born to Michael and Carole Middleton at the Royal Berkshire Hospital in Reading on 9 January 1982 and is the eldest of three children. After schooling in Amman, Jordan (where her father worked for two and a half years) and Pangbourne, she went to Marlborough College and took a gap year to travel and to study at the British Institute in Florence before enrolling at the University of St Andrew's in 2001. She graduated with a 2:1 in History of Art in 2005. Catherine then went to work in her parents' business, Party Pieces, and as a part-time buyer for the clothing company Jigsaw Junior.

From the very start Catherine Middleton was a favourite of the press. Young, beautiful and lithe of figure she was, the nation seemed to agree, 'a good catch', and after a bit of dithering, the young couple announced their engagement on Tuesday 16 November 2010.

The wedding itself was a day of national celebration. Slipping out of the Goring Hotel under a carefully placed canopy at 10.52 a.m., the bride and her father journeyed to the Abbey in a royal Rolls Royce Phantom VI and the crowd really did gasp as she emerged from the car at the Abbey, to be walked down the aisle by her father – the two of them apparently calm, collected and smiling happily.

In a dress of ivory silk and white lace designed by Sarah Burton at Alexander McQueen, Prince William's bride looked every inch the princess in a gown that took away the collective breath of the nation. After months of speculation as to what she would wear, the cat was finally out of the bag and the result was universally applauded. The bodice showed off her slender figure, and the lace appliqué that covered it was made in great secrecy by the Royal School of Needlework at Hampton Court. There was speculation as to whether or not she would wear her hair up or down, and whether or not she would wear a tiara. In the event, the hair was down and the veil held in place by a Cartier scroll tiara made in 1937 and lent to her by The Queen.

Prince William had, that morning, been created Duke of Cambridge, Earl of Strathearn and Baron Carrickfergus, and wore the uniform of Colonel of the Irish guards (at the insistence of The Queen). His best man, Prince Harry, wore the uniform of Captain of the Blues and Royals.

Prince William confessed to me that he only slept for half an hour the night before his wedding, which gave him plenty of time to plan, in his mind, the day ahead. His and Prince Harry's greatest worry on the morning of the wedding was that their spurs would cause them to trip and fall down the stairs at Clarence House!

The bride was attended by her sister, Pippa (whose svelte figure in another Sarah Burton dress awakened the nation to the alleged benefits of Pilates), and by younger brides-maids in full-skirted dresses designed and made by Nicki Macfarlane and her daughter Charlotte, while the pageboys sported Regency Footguard Officer tunics and breeches.

The couple were married by the Archbishop of Canter-bury, assisted by Richard Chartres, the Bishop of London, and in front of 1,900 guests Catherine's younger brother James read the lesson faultlessly. It was very much a family wedding. Worried that he would have to invite the list of 'dignitaries' handed to him by officials, Prince William consulted his grandmother as to what he should do. "Ask your friends first," The Queen replied. "It is your wedding."

Returning to Buckingham Palace in an open carriage, The Duke and Duchess of Cambridge waved to the cheer-ing crowds. They enjoyed a lunchtime reception and made the longed-for appearance on the palace balcony. 'The kiss' (repeated for those who missed it the first time) was beamed around the world to an estimated audience of 2 billion people in 180 countries. An estimated 5,000 street parties were held in the UK. Later in the day the couple travelled the short distance from Buckingham Palace to Clarence House in The Prince of Wales's classic Aston Martin DB6 Volante (with a sign JU5T WED attached by Prince Harry), and in the evening The Prince of Wales hosted a dinner in their honour.

The day may have passed but the vivid images remain: a smiling Michael Middleton walking his daughter down the knave of Westminster Abbey; Prince William saying, "You look beautiful," as Catherine arrived at his side; Princess Beatrice's 'pretzel' hat; the newly created Duchess of Cambridge saying, "Oh wow!" as she walked on to the balcony and saw the extent of the crowd; Prince William's three-year-old god-daughter Grace van Cutsem covering her ears on the palace balcony as the Battle of Britain Memorial Flight roared overhead; the shapely Pippa Middleton in *that* dress; and the joy on the couple's faces as they journeyed from Abbey to Palace in the open carriage waving at the thousands who had turned out to see them.

What are they like? They are exactly as they seem: pleasant, cheerful, good humoured and well aware of the nature of their responsibilities. If the success of their first official visit to Canada and the United States in 2011 is anything to

*Their first journey as a married couple took William
and Catherine down streets lined with well-wishers.*

go by, with good luck and a following wind, they'll weather the storm of publicity that will now follow them wherever they go. We can only hope and pray that they are not subjected to the degree of media intrusion that followed The Prince and Princess of Wales.

THE WEDDING OF ZARA PHILLIPS AND MIKE TINDALL

Prince William was not the only grandchild of The Queen to marry in 2011 – The Princess Royal's daughter Zara

Phillips married England rugby captain Mike Tindall in Edinburgh on 30 July. Crowds lined the streets for the first royal wedding to be held in Scotland in almost 20 years (The Princess Royal having married the then Commander Timothy Laurence at Crathie Kirk in 1992). It was very much a family wedding at Canongate Kirk on Edinburgh's Royal Mile. The bride's dress on this occasion was designed by The Queen's dressmaker Stewart Parvin and was accompanied by a pair of Jimmy Choo shoes.

THE DUKE OF EDINBURGH'S 90TH BIRTHDAY

With characteristic feistiness, The Duke was determined to avoid any kind of fuss on reaching his tenth decade. Born on 10 June 1921, his 90th birthday fell on a Friday – a normal working day as far as he was concerned (though to mark the occasion, The Queen did confer upon him the title of Lord High Admiral which, until that moment, she had held herself). There was a reception for the 100th anniversary of the Royal National Institute for Deaf People, of which he has been patron for many years, at Buckingham Palace, and in the evening he chaired a meeting of Senior Colonels in advance of the following day's Trooping the Colour ceremony, giving a dinner for them afterwards.

The Duke did, however, consent to mark his 90 years with a service at St George's Chapel on Sunday 12 June, during which the Dean of Westminster mentioned The Duke's unwillingness to take praise but said, to the sound of much laughter, that on this occasion it had to be done anyway.

Among the music chosen for the service was a setting of the 'Jubilate Deo' which had been written for the Chapel 50 years earlier by Benjamin Britten at The Duke's request. There were 800 in the congregation, and the service was followed by a champagne reception in Windsor Castle, hosted by The Queen, followed by lunch for 100 members of an 'extended' royal family.

Two television interviews were granted to mark The Duke's 90th – one to the BBC, conducted by Fiona Bruce, and one to ITV in which I myself asked the questions. To both interviewers the role presented a considerable challenge. The Duke is not an easy man to interview. Some put it down to churlishness, others to an inability to suffer fools. Having spent one hour and ten minutes endeavouring to get The Duke to talk about himself I have come to the conclusion that after 60 years of supporting The Queen he simply does not wish to push himself forward. He is, at heart, a modest man, one who sees his place as being that of staunch supporter and confidant to The Queen, but never 'out in front'. He will talk freely about things in which he is actively involved – carriage driving or the restoration of Windsor Castle – but getting him to talk about his personal life is difficult. As he admitted to me some time later, interviews are "not my favourite occupation".

The press may frequently remind us of his 'gaffes', but to most of us he is a man who has tirelessly supported The Queen for six decades, and whose sharp wit, straight talking and good humour have brought colour into our lives.

"Today, as I mark 60 years as your Queen, I am writing to thank you for the wonderful support and encouragement that you have given to me and Prince Philip over these years and to tell you how deeply moved we have been to receive so many kind messages about the Diamond Jubilee.

"In this special year, as I dedicate myself anew to your service, I hope we will all be reminded of the power of togetherness and the convening strength of family, friendship and good neighbourliness, examples of which I have been fortunate to see throughout my reign and which my family and I look forward to seeing in many forms as we travel throughout the United Kingdom and the wider Commonwealth.

"I hope also that this Jubilee year will be a time to give thanks for the great advances that have been made since 1952 and to look forward to the future with clear head and warm heart as we join together in our celebrations.

"I send my sincere good wishes to you all."

60TH ANNIVERSARY OF THE QUEEN'S ACCESSION, 2012

MAKING AN IMPRESSION

In May 2011 The Queen hosted a State Visit to Britain by President and Mrs Obama. Somewhat surprisingly it was only the second full state visit to be accorded to an American president – the first being that of President George W. Bush in 2003. The president was, said his ambassador Louis B. Susman, hugely impressed.

In October of that year The Queen and The Duke of Edinburgh enjoyed a particularly successful visit to Australia, but both these successes were eclipsed in May 2011 by the first visit to Ireland by a British sovereign since that of King George V in 1911.

The security worries about the trip were considerable, but The Queen was unshaken in her determination to celebrate the tenth anniversary of the signing of the Peace

Agreement. The Irish were split as to whether or not the trip was a wise move, and whether or not The Queen could pull it off. As she stepped from the plane wearing bright green the Irish press were smitten, and over the four days of the visit Her Majesty carried herself with dignity and humility in the face of what could have been an uneasy tour. She laid a wreath at the memorial of those who lost their lives in the fight for Irish independence, and on the following day at the memorial for the 50,000 Irishmen who laid down their lives in World War I.

There were several bomb threats but the four days passed, in the end without incident and there were two particularly remarkable moments: one at a concert given in The Queen's honour when, as she left, the entire audience stood and applauded, and the other at the state banquet at Dublin Castle when, sitting next to Irish President Mary McAleese, The Queen spoke her opening words in Gaelic: *A hUachtarain agus a chairde* – "President and friends …". These words were few, but they were significant; significant enough for the Irish president to look to her neighbour and say, "Wow!"

It was a small gesture, but a crucial one, added to by The Queen's expression of deep sympathy and regret for the lives lost in conflict over the preceding years. It proved, once more, that in certain circumstances and on certain occasions, only The Queen, by virtue of her unique position, and the manner in which she fills it, can build bridges and break down barriers. That she did both those things on her visit to Ireland is beyond dispute.

THE FUTURE

The changes The Queen has seen in her realm during the 60 years of her reign are astonishing. She has seen Commonwealth countries become independent and no doubt awaits the vote on Scottish independence with more than a little interest. But what is also astonishing is the way in which she has adapted over the decades to the changing needs of a changing population and changing values. Her own values have remained constant – a dedication to Britain and the Commonwealth founded on a secure faith and a belief in doing her duty, not ostentatiously, but consistently.

The Christmas Messages scattered through this book reveal a woman of great conviction and deep faith, devoted to her people and conscious of the difficulties that need to be overcome in life, the tragedies of war and bereavement, and the problems thrown up by differences of colour, creed and financial means. The Queen may live in a palace, a castle and fine houses, but she is not sheltered from the problems that beset her people, her ministers or her armed forces. She is brought into contact with them daily. That in her mid eighties she continues to shoulder the burden of state so diligently is a tribute to her conviction as well as her stamina.

When she does eventually relinquish the role of sovereign, at the time of God's choosing, not her own, The Prince of Wales will become King. Never before will there have been a monarch who knows his country or the world better than he does, or indeed who has in his time as heir to the throne done more to make a difference for the better. He is one of the world's greatest charitable entrepreneurs, raising in excess of £100 million a year to support the charities he has started, which are invariably causes which would otherwise be overlooked.

Yes, The Prince of Wales does become involved in initiatives that can irritate those in high places in the business and architectural world. Yes, he is vocal on those issues he sees as important and where he believes he can make a difference – from conserving red squirrels to securing the future of Dumfries House in Scotland and providing social housing in run-down areas. But there is no shortage of people – especially young people – who will tell you that without his intervention they would not have had the encouragement and incentive to make something of their lives – whether it is by starting up a business or training in a particular skill.

Over the last 25 years I have had the pleasure and privilege of working with The Prince on a number of projects. He is a remarkable man, who has had to forge his own path in a unique role for which there is no job description. It would be perfectly possible, and, indeed, entirely in keeping with his predecessors, for him to have done very little as heir to the throne but enjoy the trappings of his position. This has not been his way. For over 30 years he has served his country with a sense of duty and great courage. It won him no friends talking about climate change and the need to care for the environment in the 1970s, or to be raising concerns about disadvantaged young people, the quality of education or the standards of some modern architecture, the plight of farmers or the poor quality of food being fed to our children and those in hospital. He suffered – and continues to suffer – attacks when he speaks out. Edward VIII, who was King for such a short time, famously visited Welsh mining communities in 1936 just before he abdicated. He was shocked by what he saw and said, "Something must be done." His great nephew says exactly the same thing but goes a step further: "Something must be done – and I will do it." I asked him once why he felt the need to become involved in so many causes. His answer was simple and heartfelt: "Because I mind. And if I can make a difference then it would be criminal not to."

I'm very happy to count The Prince of Wales and The Duchess of Cornwall as friends. You could argue that this may colour my judgement; but I've seen at first hand the difference they can make and the joy they bring to the folk who meet them.

What I know for certain is that The Prince of Wales has the same sense of duty and commitment to this country and its people as The Queen and should be judged on his unique set of achievements. Those achievements are not inconsiderable and have often been undertaken in the face of heavy criticism. He could have given in, taken the path of least resistance and gone quietly, or simply devoted his energies to having a good time, as some of his predecessors chose to do. He did not. He stuck at it and continues to do so, tirelessly, day in, day out.

I know of no one who works harder, no one who is more committed and no one who is more devoted to Britain and its people. And as we head into the 61st year of The Queen's reign we would do well to appreciate that and to be thankful that, after her, God willing, will come a King every bit as conscientious and dedicated to the needs of his people as Queen Elizabeth II. May God bless them both.

The Queen and the future King – two of the most hard working,
dedicated monarchs a nation could hope for.

INDEX

PICTURE CREDITS

ACKNOWLEDGEMENTS

Where to begin? Over the years I have been privileged to meet almost every member of the royal family, and while conversations and interviews were not recorded or undertaken with the specific aim of writing this book they have given me an insight into the workings of monarchy and, in some cases, into their opinions.

This is not intended as a book of stupendous revelations. It is an unashamedly sympathetic book but one which I hope still informs, evaluates, entertains and gives an overview of how monarchy interacts with the man and woman in the street as well as with the government of the day, and how our own lives, as well as that of The Queen, have changed over the last sixty years.

Interviews with Their Royal Highnesses The Prince of Wales, The Duke of Cambridge, The Duke of York, The Duke of Edinburgh, The Princess Royal, Princess Eugenie and The Earl of Wessex have informed my opinions and I am enormously grateful for their patience and good humour in answering questions on a variety of topics.

My thanks are due to Sue Phillips for research, to Lorna Russell, Joe Cottington and Caroline McArthur for editorial advice and also to Imogen Fortes and Claire Scott.